26/11/22.

To Dear Ais...
Thank you ...
attending my ...

I Love You Because...

loves
Evelyn

Evelyn Killeen McCrann

Evelyn Killeen McCrann

May you receive much
enjoyment, laughter and smiles...

... as your read through the
book. xx.

Cover Design and Interior Formatting:
Dorothy Dreyer.
Editor: Niall MacGiolla Bhuí,
TheDocCheck.Com

ISBN: 978-1-7391012-1-3

Published by Book Hub Publishing, An Independent Publishing House,
Galway and Limerick, Ireland.
www.bookhubpublishing.com

*Book Hub Publishing uses paper sourced from sustainable forestry. We are committed to inclusion and diversity.

Table of contents

I love you Because

I love you because you understand, dear
Every single thing I try to do.
You're always there to lend a helping hand, dear.
I love you most of all because you're you.

No matter what the world may say about me,
I know your love will always see me through
I love you for the way you never doubt me
But most of all I love you 'cause you're you.

I love you because my heart is lighter
Every time I'm walking by your side
I love you because the future's brighter
The door to happiness, you open wide.

No matter what the world may say about you me
I know your love will always see me through
I love you for a hundred thousand reasons
But most of all I love you 'cause you're you…

Written by Leon Roger Payne
Released in 1964 by Jim Reeves

Short Stories

'The Importance of Waiting'

Short listed for Roscommon New writing Award 2020
Dedicated to Gertie, Majella and Josephine

They left their Raleigh racers against the windowsill of the two bedroomed cottage on main Street. Madge knocked on the faded front door.

"Tommy, it's Madge and Gertrude," stated Gertrude, banging briskly and loudly to make sure he could hear her. Tommy was a widower who lived on his own. He enjoyed his weekly visit from members of the Legion of Mary. It was unusual for him not to be at home at eight pm. Gertrude decided to peer through the cobwebbed windowpane. She could not see him but again called out,

"Tommy, … He's not here," she sighed.

"Sure, we'll wait a few minutes, Gertrude. He can't be gone too far."

Gertrude had already waited half an hour at Kelly's corner

for Madge. She did not show up so she decided to fly on her racer to Madge's flat. She had forgotten all about the visit. She admitted she had just got out of bed after treating herself to an evening nap. Gertrude waited again to give her time to get dressed.

"*Time is Time*" her father's repetitive phrase flashed into her mind. She wasn't waiting any longer for Tommy.

"I'm going home, Madge," she announced.

"Oh no you're not, he's coming behind you," she smiled.

Tommy had taken advantage of the magnificent sunny May evening and was returning home after a short stroll.

"How are ye, girleens?" he asked, smiling, as he approached them slowly due to a slight limp and advanced years.

"Come on in," he added, turning the key in his cottage door. They followed him into his modest kitchen.

During their hourly visit, they usually offered him help with his household chores. He always insisted on making them a cup of tea while they revealed the latest news from around the market town. And during every visit, Tommy would always recall memories of his dear wife who had passed away a few years previously. On this visit, Madge took a long look at the Stanley range.

"Tommy, I'm going to give that range a good cleaning," she said.

"Fair enough, Madge," agreed Tommy.

"Now what could I clean it with?" she asked herself out loud, as Tommy's cleaning agents were minimal.

"What about Quix washing up liquid?" suggested Gertrude.

Madge suddenly spotted a lump of lard on Tommy's oil clothed kitchen table.

"This will do the trick," she said excitedly.

Tommy suggested making them both a cup of tea as they began their cleaning duties.

"Hold on until we are finished cleaning Tommy. It won't take too long," asserted Gertrude.

Madge dropped the square block of lard onto the top of the hot Stanley range and started to move it around with a knife that she had stuck in the middle of it. The lard started to spit and bubble as it burst across the top of the range, taking on a life of its own. Suddenly, smoke started to ascend, higher and higher aiming towards the already grey ceiling. Like an infectious disease, it spread fast through the room. All three of them began to cough and sneeze and darkness began to descend over Tommy's kitchen.

"O my god Madge, you'll set the house on fire" said Gertrude in a frightened voice.

"Don't worry, it's only smoke caused by the dirt and ashes on the range Gertrude. There will be no fire," she assured her.

Gertrude had seen her mother use lard when she was making pastry but she never saw her use it to clean a Stanley range or anything else for that matter.

"Well, I never saw my mother…" Tommy interrupted her. "Will you go over and open the front door a Grá and I'll open this window beside me. The smoke will be gone in no time," he said politely. Gertrude made a dash to open the front door wide and then ran out to the scullery to open the back door too.

Tommy was sitting at the kitchen table, his favourite spot in the cottage. The window, located beside him, looked out onto the main street, giving him the opportunity to watch the world go by. It was here he sat every day not only to have his meals but also to say the rosary while looking up at the Sacred Heart picture which hung over the kitchen table.

Gertrude felt embarrassed and annoyed by the incident but said nothing. She did not want to upset poor Tommy or spoil her close relationship with Madge. Madge, now in her thirties and Tommy in his late seventies had a bit more life experience and wisdom so she decided to accept that they knew best. Gertrude was an excitable nineteen-year-old with not a care in the world, not even for the shorthand and typing exams which she was about to undertake a couple of weeks later.

After waiting patiently for the smoke to fly through the doors and window and for the dust and dirt to 'lie down' on every inch of the kitchen, Madge blurted out,

"I'll keep cleaning the Stanley range, Gertrude. It will look like span new by the time I'm finished with it."

"Fair enough," Gertrude replied. She then began to think about where or what she would start to clean first. There was no time to waste because the cleaning time was going to take much longer now than usual.

"Girleens, would you like some music to listen to while you work?" Tommy suggested.

"Not a bad idea," Gertrude answered, pouring boiling water into the rectangular red basin used for washing the delph. The battery-operated transistor sat on the worn oil clothed kitchen table.

"You can choose the station yourself Gertrude," Tommy chuckled.

Gertrude turned on the radio. It was set at RTE Radio one. "We won't get the Top Ten hits on this station Tommy," she joked.

"I don't think Tommy has any interest in the Top Ten, Gertrude," declared Madge.

"You'd be surprised," Gertrude answered, looking up to see her overstretching her arm cleaning the ceiling with an old shirt while standing on Tommy's creaky fireside armchair.

"Ah, Madge, be careful; we don't want any more incidents or accidents. Tie the shirt around the sweeping brush instead. You won't have to do any stretching then," she advised her.

Gertrude continued to fiddle with the needle on the

transistor, searching slowly for the popular pirate British radio station known as Radio Caroline. At last, she found it.

"Got myself a crying, talkin', sleepin', walkin', living doll..."

The chorus of the song Living Doll was playing. Cliff Richard's song was a number one hit for many weeks now and one of her favourite songs to dance to that year of 1986. She turned up the volume and continued to sing along.

"Got to do my best to please her just 'cos she's a livin' doll..."

"What do you think of this new number one hit, Tommy?"

"New? sure, that was a hit when I was a young lad."

"Well how about stepping out here, Tommy, and we'll have a dance."

She held him steady as they gently moved around the kitchen floor helping him to keep time to the music.

"Take a look at her hair, it's real, if you don't believe what I say..."

"We'll be here 'till midnight with the way you're carrying on, Gertrude," interrupted Madge.

"Ah sure, we're only having a bit of fun. Don't worry, we'll get the cleaning done," Gertrude assured her.

"That's true," admitted Madge, moving to the rhythm of the music while dusting the old mahogany sideboard.

During a break from their cleaning, Tommy informed them over a cup of tea and digestive biscuits that he could never forget that song. It was a big hit in the summer of 1959. It was also the year he and his late wife Kathleen celebrated their twenty-fifth wedding anniversary. That was twenty-seven years ago, and it was plain to see that she was still very much alive in his heart.

Radio Caroline continued to hurl out the hits that evening as they continued cleaning until the late hours. Waiting the hour for Madge and waiting for Tommy to arrive home was important. It gave Gertrude the opportunity to give of her time, her friendship and care to someone in need. The evening had been an eventful one, an evening full of enjoyment, excitement and entertainment for all three of them, especially Tommy. It was an evening Gertrude would never forget. She had realised the importance of waiting.

'All For the Sake of a Party'

Dedicated to Marie Keane

She stood there looking at them, tapping her chin, wondering what she would do. It was Friday evening. The party was on Monday. She had left it too late to dry clean them. "Will I take a chance and put them into the washing machine?" she asked herself out loud. Her mother would never dream of doing such a thing. They had been part of the family home for over fifty years and now Mary was thinking about taking a chance, a chance that may destroy the thick luxurious curtains.

"They were bought in Lanigan's drapers on main street soon after we got married!" her mother often boasted and emphasised that they had cost quite a penny at the time.

The cost of them may have been one reason that her children only saw the full-length tomato red curtains at Christmas time or when the family took their turn to have the village station mass. The two lonely pairs hung in the sitting room for over thirty years. Then, they took up their new residence following the building of a much-needed extension to the family home. The new Livingroom displayed a much larger window that looked out onto the front garden. Her mother could not bear to part with her much-loved curtains. She came up with the creative idea of sewing the two pairs of curtains together to make one larger pair for the new window. She knew the helpful neighbour Betty was the right person to carry out the task. Betty was considered a genius when it came to sewing and knitting.

Mary was no genius though when it came to the self-cleaning of curtains but made the decision that Friday evening to push the thick curtains in the washing machine. Mary's mother was staying with her sister that weekend so she would never know, or be told of her mad decision. She placed one pair at a time into the washing machine, turning the dial to a 'quick 30.'

No harm can come to them at such a low temperature, she believed.

She later called on her husband to lift the now much heavier curtains onto the clothesline.

"John," she called out loudly as she stood in the pantry facing the washing machine. There was no answer. She turned on her heel and walked briskly into the living room where John was reading the daily newspaper sitting beside the open fire.

"Did you not hear me calling you?" she asked.

"No," he replied. "What's wrong?" he continued.

"I need your help to lift the curtains onto the clothes line," she stated.

"Can you not wait until I finish reading the newspaper?"

"No, sure it will only take a few minutes," she insisted.

Letting out a deep sigh, he dropped the newspaper and followed her out to the pantry. Together they carried the curtains out to the backyard and stretched them neatly along the wired clothes line, placing the pegs neatly along the curtain lining. Mary took another look at them.

"I don't think they have shrunk, what do you think, John?"

"Ah, I wouldn't have a clue to tell you the truth," he answered.

The following morning upon waking, Mary pulled back the curtains of the rear bedroom window at her family home.

"Oh no," she screeched. "John, John, wake up". All she could hear back was a deep moan.

Heavy rain had poured throughout the night and managed to weigh down the curtains to the ground. She let out another roar at John.

"Get up quick."

"What's wrong," he asked in a sleepy voice.

"The curtain, the curtains," she shouted.

"There's no need to shout, I'm right beside you, Mary."

She didn't wait to explain any further. In her fur lined slippers and brand-new nightgown, she raced through the house and out through the back kitchen door to find out what damage had been done. Staring at the curtains, she noticed the red dye of the fabric had spread like ink onto the thick lining. They were now a baby pink. The rain-soaked curtains were now mottled with green moss, blackened with dirt and engrained with gravel.

"Oh why did I bother at all?" she wailed out loud.

"What was I thinking of, washing curtains all for the sake of a party? Why didn't I check the forecast?" she asked herself out loud with frustration.

John was now standing at the back door looking at her, yawning.

"I suppose I better help you lift them back up onto the line," he said.

"For what? Sure, what is the point, they're destroyed now," she said and she began to cry.

"Destroyed, what do you mean by destroyed?"

"Well just take a look at them, they are soaking wet, covered in dirt and the lining is now pink from the dye of the curtains. I'll have to dump them and buy a new pair for the party," she explained to him.

"Please stop panicking, Mary," he replied in a calm voice. "The answer is simple," he added.

"Simple?" she repeated in an agitated tone.

"Yes, simple. First of all, do not dump those precious curtains. If you do, it's curtains for you. Your mother would never forgive you and secondly you could forget about having the party. Instead, leave them out on the line until they have dried because according to this weekend's weather forecast, a very strong breeze is promised," he informed her.

Her tears stopped suddenly and she began to smile. They lifted the filthy extra heavy curtains back on the line, putting extra wooden pegs in place to avoid a second disaster.

A strong westerly breeze later blew through the antique curtains as predicted, removing all traces of dirt, moss and gravel. No evidence was left to show that the spring-cleaned curtains had been through 'hell and high water' over the weekend. Mary would be forever thankful for her dear husband's advice.

That Monday evenging, her mother's curtains hung beautifully on the Livingroom window looking and feeling better than ever before. The lining was still tinged with pink but no one would notice. They were ready to show themselves off to family, neighbours and friends who would attend her mother's surprise eightieth birthday party.

'Anything can Happen'

Marie stood at her cream kitchen counter. Her hands, which seemed to be ever covered in flour, began to roll the pastry over and back with her well used rolling pin. One of her favourite songs "From the Candy Store on the Corner," a smash hit for the popular showband leader Dicky Rock began to play on the transistor radio which was located close by.

"From the Candy store on the corner..." She loved that song and couldn't help but join in. *"To the Chapel on the hill, two young lovers are longing to go there..."*

She was keeping time to the music as she rolled out the orange flavoured pastry for her famous apple tarts. She was unaware that her husband, Mossie had entered the kitchen. He silently watched her with amusement. He knew why the song meant a lot to her as it reached number one on the day she celebrated her 21st birthday. Mossie himself loved the song and sang it to his wife over the years, especially when they were courting. He now needed to catch her attention and the only way of doing so was to go over and turn down the radio. Marie immediately turned her head to see her husband of thirty years standing in front of her.

"Gosh, Mossie, you gave me an awful fright. I was in another world. I was thinking back to my younger days when I first heard that song."

Mossie took a good look around the kitchen. He could see no sign of his tea approaching. All he could see was cooked apple tarts, raw apple tarts and raw pastry.

"Where's my tea? I'm starving!" he announced.

He was about to take up a knife to cut a slice of one of the apple tarts when his wife quickly responded that they were for a special occasion. Mossie didn't know what she meant by a 'special occasion.' He often admitted that he was never a great man for remembering special dates like birthdays and anniversaries. And it looked like he had forgotten a major anniversary on this occasion.

She walked over to him and stood looking into his olive-green eyes for a few moments before asking him the question.

"What were you doing this day thirty years ago?"

"Thirty years ago," he laughed. "I can hardly remember what I was doing last week," he replied.

"Ah come on now, how could you forget our wedding anniversary? Thirty years of wedded bliss!"

"O god, I'm sorry, Marie, I totally forgot all about it." he answered, feeling embarrassed.

Marie didn't take it to heart for she knew that when she did remind him, he always made it up to her with a special treat.

However, Mossie was a quiet, reserved man who shunned the lime light, so when he heard that Marie was organizing a party in the house later that night to celebrate the event, he showed no enthusiasm.

"There's no need for that at all. We'll go out for dinner just the two of us during the week," he suggested.

And then he quickly changed the subject wanting to know when his tea going to be ready as he walked over to the oven to check if there was a grill being kept warm for him.

"There's no tea for you," came Marie's swift reply as she walked towards the kitchen door.

She had no time as she was about to make sandwiches with the help of her neighbours who were coming to the party.

"Where are you going now love?" he asked in an anxious voice.

"I'm going to the car to bring in the groceries," she told him.

Poor Mossie thought she was joking about the party. Now he knew she was serious. He had a more relevant reason why this party could not go ahead. He wondered how he going to explain the reason to his wife. But he didn't wonder for long when it came to relieving his starvation, as he quickly grabbed one of the tarts and a knife and ran with them to their bedroom. He cut a slice and stuffed it into his mouth before placing it under the bed as he had done many times before. He returned to the kitchen to find Marie emptying out the contents of two canvas bags full with bread, butter, ham, chicken, cheese and lettuce.

"Come on now, pet, and help me make a few fresh sandwiches. Then all three of us can sit down and have a cup of tea and we will tell you more about the 'surprise' night ahead."

"Three of us, what do you mean?"

"Well, your dear son Oliver will be arriving home soon," she stated.

Mossie shook his head and slowly announced, "Ah… he won't be coming over."

Marie looked at her husband in confusion.

"What do you mean? Sure, he has to come. Oliver and his friends are providing the entertainment for us tonight and of course he will be playing the tin whistle."

"He won't be," Mossie insisted.

All of this did not make sense to Marie as she focussed on her husband's facial expression. She knew him long enough to know that there was something he was holding back.

"That feckin' tin whistle of his," Mossie blurted out.

"Sorry, what did you say?"

"Ah. nothing," came his reply and then he decided to tell a little white lie.

"He can't come, he has a date."

Marie would have known if their only son had a date and if he had, he certainly would not have picked today, his mother and father's anniversary. She knew there was something going on and she needed to find out quickly what it was.

Mossie was stubborn and continued to tell her that there was nothing going on.

"Well, nothing means something, Mossie, so out with it."

"That tin whistle of his is going to get him into awful bother some day!"

Marie wondered what had the tin whistle got to do with it? He had caught him at it again. Before he could tell his wife anymore, he asked her to take a seat at the kitchen table. He was going to tell her the full story.

Mossie informed his bewildered wife Marie that when was driving home from work the previous day along the dual carriage way, he spotted a familiar van passing him out in the fast lane. He realised that it was their son Oliver in the van. He was playing his tin whistle while he had his van placed in cruise control. He immediately rang him to tell him to take the whistle out of his mouth before the gardai caught up with him. But before he finished talking, his son hung up on him.

He waited anxiously to hear his wife's reaction. And it

wasn't what he had expected.

"Sure, he was only getting in some practice for tonight's session," she laughed.

Mossie couldn't get over his wife's reaction.

"Practicing, you mean practicing to get points on his licence, or worse a fine and maybe put off the road for a few years," he stated.

"Calm down, Mossie. That won't stop him from turning up for our anniversary and he definitely won't miss out on his mammy's apple tart."

No sooner had she the words out of her mouth when they both heard the horn of Oliver's van blowing.

"Didn't I tell you, love, that he would be over," she said, with a broad smile.

Oliver arrived into the kitchen playing an appropriate tune on his tin whistle for his parent's anniversary called "Marie's Wedding."

Marie couldn't help herself as she burst into song again.

"Step we gaily, on we go
Heel for heel and toe for toe
Arm in arm and row and row…"

And tried her best at the same time to swing her husband around the kitchen to cheer him up.

When the tune was over, Oliver returned the tin whistle to the inside of his sock on his right leg. He quickly greeted his parents with a big hug to celebrate their special day. He then placed his right arm lovingly around his father's shoulder and jokingly said.

"Have you calmed down, daddy? Gosh you were in some state yesterday."

Marie quickly changed the subject and asked them both to help make a few sandwiches before sitting down to have them with a fresh cup of tea followed by a slice of her tasty apple tart.

Oliver began to praise his mother's wonderful baking as he counted five tarts.

"Five," repeated his mother. "I made six. where is the other one?" Her eyes immediately focused on her son.

"Well don't look at me, mammy. I've just arrived," and he started to walk towards the hallway telling her he will be back in a jiffy.

"How well do you know daddy?" he asked his mother a couple of minutes later as he arrived into the kitchen holding an apple tart behind his back.

"Ah better than himself," she replied.

He then held out the apple tart in front of her.

"Well, you obviously don't know everything about him after thirty years as he has a bad habit of hiding apple tarts under your bed so that he has something to eat when he gets hungry."

"Well, there's no doubt about it, anything can happen around here," laughed Marie.

"Sure, there's nothing wrong or silly about that," blushed Mossie.

"Nothing at all, daddy, no sillier than playing a tin whistle while driving a car in cruise control."

"I wonder want will happen next?" asked Marie jokingly to her husband and son.

As they began to make a variety of neatly cut sandwiches, Mossie could not help but ask if he was bringing Ann to the party.

"Ann, o no, she's long gone, I'm dating Nollaig now, dad," he said with a giant smile across his face. And continued to boast to his parents that he met her on New Year's Eve at a party.

"Who is Nollaig? … You are dating her eight months, son. And you never told us? How did you manage to keep the romance quiet for so long?"

"Well, I wanted to make sure I had the right woman this time, dad."

"The right woman! What do you mean by that, Oliver?"

Mossie looked at his wife and then looked at their son.

Marie burst out, "Son, are you planning to make this girl your wife?"

"Yes, Mammy, how did you guess?"

"Oh Ollie, I just knew by the glint in your eye. I'm so delighted for you," she said throwing her arms around her son and planting a big kiss on this cheek.

"Isn't this wonderful news, Moss, what exciting news to hear on our wedding anniversary."

"Hold on a minute," interrupted Mossie.

"I hope you are not planning to propose to her tonight at the party, sure we haven't even met her yet, son."

Oliver let out a loud laugh.

"Ah, daddy, you are panicking again over nothing. Of course, I don't plan to propose to Nollaig tonight. This is your special night. A night to celebrate your thirty happy married years together and all the years living with you two loving and caring parents. I just felt this would be the perfect night to introduce Nollaig to you both."

"Did you hear that, Moss? Aren't we so lucky to have such a kind hearted son?"

"You are right there, love. You are a wonderful son Oliver."

"Now, Mammy and Daddy, before the neighbours and friends arrive to help you get this party started, what tune would you both like for me to play for your first dance tonight?"

Moss and Marie knew instantly what it was going to be as they called out together 'Candy Store on the Corner'.

And they both burst into their favourite verse from the song in celebration of their thirty years together.

"At seventeen it's a thrill to dream some day they will
Walk hand in hand from the candy store
To the chapel on the hill."

Are You SURE You Want to Stay in the Class?

Dedicated to all my school friends and remembering the fun times we had back in the 1980s

She knew she wasn't a contender for college. And so, she wondered what could she do with herself for the coming year.

"Would you consider the shorthand and typing course in the Tech?" asked Eithne. "We'll even get paid for it," she continued.

"Shorthand and typing" Eileen repeated. "Me, a secretary! I can't see me or you taking up such a job. Sure, we don't even have the look of one. Can you ever see us locked up in an office banging away on a typewriter?"

"No," assured Eithne.

However, after a short silence, Eileen boldly stated, "We'll do it. It's not every day you get paid to do a course and it means another year together, another year full of fun and mischief."

Eileen had zero interest in the mechanical writing machine. Pure penance it was, practicing typing all those letters.

"Don't look down" was the rule that was drilled into them each day by Ms. O' Connor. And the shorthand, well did she suffer? She couldn't, for the life of her, get to grips with the many symbols she had to learn off by heart, never mind writing them with speed while taking down notes. Eileen was not prepared to suffer for much longer. A different attitude was needed… FAST.

Her attitude changed fairly lively one weary Wednesday in November when Eileen exclaimed, "Could you please slow down Miss Kelly? You are going too fast!" She had been reading a short paragraph out loud to the class and timing it as the students wrote down the information.

"Eileen, are you SURE you want to stay in the class?" she asked letting out a long sigh.

"Yes, Miss," Eileen replied immediately, even though she wanted to give her a very different answer. Eileen was never going to be a typist, secretary, call it what you damn well like. Eileen and Eithne decided to focus their attention on what THEY would get up to between classes; morning breaks and lunch breaks. THEY, included, the bold Martine McDermott and Mairead Ni Doláin. Those two were fit for any devilment. They would say or do anything during class to vex the teachers and amuse the students.

By May, things were very getting serious. Both teachers were trying to emphasise the importance of practicing shorthand and typewriting speed. The word "practice, practice, practice" was hammered into their ears.

"Has anyone got a typewriter at home they could practice on?" asked Ms. O' Connor, the Friday before the final exams.

Martine McDermott put up her hand. All heads turned towards her. What was she about to say?

"Miss, I have an ould typewriter at the house but I've run out of ribbon roll. Would you mind giving me one roll so that I can practice typing over the weekend please? I want to perfect my speed."

"You mean a ribbon spool, Martine," corrected Ms. O' Connor.

Eileen looked at Eithne. Both of them shook their heads because they knew McDermott didn't possess a typewriter at home.

"What is she up to?" wondered Eithne.

"Not much, I can assure you," replied Eileen as they continued to watch the drama unfold. Ms. O'Connor's face beamed. She was thrilled with Martine's enthusiasm.

"Of course, you can have a spool, Martine."

A bigger smile stretched across Martine's face as she watched the skinny fingered teacher opened her desk drawer to locate the ribbon spool.

"Good on you, Martine," she said and planted the spool into her hand. Suddenly, there were whispers going on between McDermott and Ni Doláin.

Eithne whispered to Eileen. "Those two are planning something. I know by the look of them." The lunch bell rang.

Lunch time was usually spent quickly devouring lunches so that most of the lunch break could be devoted to down town where they would be admired by fellas they fancied. Lads blowing car horns, offering car spins, whistling and waving at the women through open car windows was a daily occurrence. Eileen quickly stood up from her desk and rushed to get her lunch box from the corner of the classroom. Suddenly, Martine and Mairead approached her on either side.

"We have a special lunch treat for ya, Eileen," said Martine.

"Really, girls," she replied excitedly. Mairead suddenly grabbed hold of Eileen and held her tight while Martine produced the famous ribbon spool and began to wrap the ribbon around Eileen's neck. Around and around, she went with it. Eileen began to scream. "Stop…Stop." Mairead and Martine had now begun to rub the ink into her neck. Eileen's screams put the fear of God in them and the rest of the class. They would all be suspended if caught. Everyone made a dash out the classroom door, all but one student, Eithne Murphy.

Pulling Eileen by the arm, Eithne said, "Come with me quick into the toilets, we've got to get that off your neck before Ms. Kelly arrives."

Eithne wanted to scream with laughter as she observed her friend staring in the mirror. Her neck was now black as her bobbed haircut. 'This is all we have, Eileen," he told her as she lifted the Carbolic soap which sat on the sink in the bathroom.

She rolled up her sleeves and, using sheets and sheets of toilet paper and soap, she began the operation to remove all evidence of the black ink from Eileen's neck. Eithne's operation was a success. The ink was gone from her neck but the inside of her white uniformed blouse collar was destroyed so Eileen buttoned up the blouse tight around her neck to hide the black blobs.

The school bell rang again. Lunch break was over. Ms. Kelly arrived promptly to class and began her daily student roll call.

"Martine McDermott." No answer.

She stared down at the class. She could see that her neighbour, Ms Ni Doláin was not to be seen either.

"Does anybody know of the whereabouts of these two ladies?"

"No miss," the class chimed together.

"They probably think we reported them so they're afraid to come back to class," Eileen whispered to Eithne.

"Eileen Grogan, do you know where these two ladies are?"

"No miss," answered Eileen.

Suddenly, the classroom door burst open.

"Sorry miss, we're late. We had to help a man find his way to a house on the Athlone Road so we got into his lorry and gave him directions," explained Mairead.

"Excuse me?" replied Ms. Kelly.

"It was a Roadstone lorry, miss, and your man hadn't a clue where the address was but I knew where it was so he asked us to hop in and show him the way. He promised he would give us a lift back to school afterwards. So that is why we are late," explained Martine, showing off a proud smile.

"What? He could have been Jack the Ripper. Don't ever do that again. Sit down," she ordered.

Martine then started to sing the song, "The Greatest Love of All" which was the number one hit in the charts that week.

"Are you SURE you want to stay in the class Ms. McDermott?" stated Ms Kelly using a stern tone.

"Of course, miss."

Roars of laughter filled the classroom.

"That's enough class," added Ms. Kelly.

"What will those two get up next, Eileen?" whispered Eithne.

"Something tells me there's more to come," said Eileen taking a bite out of a banana as she had no time to eat her lunch.

"Ms. Murphy, take out your Pitman shorthand dictionary… And put away that banana Ms. Grogan. Lunch is long over," ordered Ms. Kelly.

"Ok miss," they replied in unison.

Another week was over. Eileen could not wait to get out of the school building and get on her bike. She needed fresh air and she needed food.

Eileen and Eithne headed towards the bike shed to collect their Raleigh bicycles. From a distance, Eileen noticed that there was something attached to her bike. Eileen was short-sighted.

Eithne was longsighted.

"Oh no, they have done it again."

"Done what again, Eithne?"

They were standing now in front of the bikes. Eileen was staring at hers.

"What in the name of God...How am I going to get home?" she wailed.

Endless typewriter ribbon had been wound around the spokes of Eileen's bike. Eithne was now holding her stomach with her left hand and holding her right hand over her mouth.

"What's wrong with you?" said Eileen.

"Oh Eileen, I can't hold it in any longer," as she began to screech with laughter and then tears began to roll down her face. Eithne's laughter was contagious. They were both now laughing loudly.

"What will you say to McDermott and Ni Doláin on Monday, Eileen?" she asked after gaining some composure.

"What can I say to them, Eithne? They gave the class some laughter today. Sure, isn't that why we did the course, so we could have fun and get up to mischief?"

"True," said Eileen.

"And admit it now Eileen, you're full of mischief yourself. We won't ever forget the time you sent a letter into the Farmers Journal pretending to be Martine looking for a man,' Eithne smirked.

"O sure I know I am, Eithne."

"Well, we have to agree that we didn't learn much shorthand and typing this year, but we sure know now creative ways to use a typewriter ribbon spool. All we need now is to figure out a creative way to undo that ribbon from your bike," laughed Eithne.

'The Grateful Neighbour'

Jim Hanley had farmed all his working life. He worked the small farm of 40 acres which his late father passed on to him. He was an only child and had never married. Now in his 70th year, he was well used to his own company, spending most of his daily life talking to his few cows, sheep and his sheep dog, Lassie. His close neighbour, Mrs Kennedy, a young widow for some years now who lived down the boreen called to visit him on a regular basis to make sure that he was ok. She never forgot to bring him some of her fresh home baking.

On entering his white pebble dashed cottage in the evenings, she would be greeted with his usual contrary 'hello.' Tom found it difficult to make conversation, even with Maura. She had become used to his grumpiness and would often catch him sitting by the open fire place, sometimes peeling tobacco with his pocket knife, listening to the radio, or sometimes just resting after a hard day's work on the farm.

"How's she cuttin', Jim?" she would ask him cheerfully.

"Ah I'm alright, Maura, I could be better," he would reply.

He would automatically go over and press on the kettle and take a sharp knife out of the drawer found underneath the tea-stained kitchen sink. He would then lay it on the kitchen table, ready to cut into the freshly baked brown bread, scone or slice of apple tart that Maura baked for him. While having the cup of tea and fresh baking with him, Maura Kennedy, a humorous lady by nature, would try to amuse him with her latest stories from the village. However, it was hard work. She found it very difficult to get a smile on poor Jim's face.

Last Tuesday evening, Maura arrived to the red coloured back door of Jim's cottage. She noticed the door was wide open which she thought it was unusual and so she called out to him,

"Jim, it's Maura, I'm here."

She received no reply. She loudly knocked on the door as she felt it was not appropriate to walk straight in. Again, there was no reply. She decided to walk in to his tiny back kitchen then through to main kitchen. There, in front of her, was Jim sitting by the Stanley range, tied to the chair. Blood trickled down his face. She ran over to him and began to shake him as her heart beat loudly.

"Jim, Jim, please wake up," she cried. She searched her coat pocket for her mobile phone.

"O no, she screamed, I left it behind me. O help me God," she pleaded.

She was drawn to Jim's bloody face. Suddenly, his deep blue eyes opened. A broad smile stretched across his face.

"You're alive, Jim," she said with relief.

She suddenly remembered his pen knife. She ran to the back kitchen and grabbed the black sharp penknife from the window sill. She raced back to him to cut through the twine to release poor Jim.

"Jim, where is your mobile phone, I left mine at home?"

"What do you need the phone for, Maura?"

"Sure, I need to ring your doctor to get him to call over and have you checked out. You're bleeding from the nose. I need to make sure that you are ok. You could have suffered a heart attack and I'd never forgive myself. I knew I should have bought you an alarm bracelet and this might never have happened," she blurted out.

"Not at all, Maura, I'm grand. I know you mean well. Come on, take a look at me. It's only a nose bleed for God's sake. I must have passed out with the shock. A neat hot brandy will sort me out."

Maura couldn't help but laugh at his reaction. She took a look around the kitchen; a few drawers had been pulled out and items sprawled on the black and white tiled kitchen floor. Had any money been stolen from the poor man she wondered?

"Do you have any money hidden in the house, Jim?" feeling a bit awkward about having to ask the question.

His eyes looked directly at Maura.

"No one will find any money in a drawer, under the floor boards or in a tin box in my cottage. Are ya joking me or what, Maura? I'm far too cute for that," he informed her.

Jim then went silent for a few moments. He seemed to be deep in thought. Suddenly he announced,

"Maura, there is something I want to tell you. I was going to let you wait under after I passed away to find out but after all the kindness you have shown to me over the years and now after this incident, I think you deserve to know it now."

Mary's coffee brown eyes zoomed in on Jim's. What was he about to say to her? she wondered.

"I made a deed with my solicitor and I didn't make it yesterday or last week I can tell you. I made a deed because it can't be changed unlike a will. You shall be the owner of this cottage and the 40 acres that come with it when I pass from this world."

Maura stood frozen on the spot; she could not believe what she was hearing. She never wanted or expected anything from the man whom she enjoyed visiting, baking for and doing little chores for him over the years. Her motto had always been that one should never do anything for anyone if one was expecting to get something back. She was only too delighted to help anyone that was in need.

"O Jim, please, there was no need to do that. I don't know how I can repay you back."

"Repay me," he repeated. "I have never told you this before but you are the sister I never had. Thank you for everything and sorry for been contrary and grumpy at times. I can't help it. I can be stubborn, and I know I'm set in my ways."

The tears started to drip down Maura's cheeks. She never realised until now how much he meant to her.

"Now, don't be getting all emotional on me. Get the brandy bottle out from the corner press and let's make a toast, a toast to grateful and generous neighbours."

"Well, Jim, she added, there is one thing I'm going to do to repay you whether you like it or not. I'm ordering an alarm bracelet for you no later than today," as she began to pour the neat Hennessy brandy into the two glasses.

"Alright, Maura, I will agree to that." He began his toast. "To good health and safety in our homes and to you my fabulous neighbour as Tina Turner's song says, 'You're simply the best'," and he loudly clinked the side of his brandy glass against hers.

'Love Comes After a Fall'

Although Margaret was now in her late thirties, she was still hopeful that the love of her life was 'just around the corner' She met her latest boyfriend at a horse race meeting and was delighted that they shared a common hobby.

'This is a good start,' she thought.

Their relationship was kept top secret. All date nights took place far away from the local village where she resided. When anyone asked her where she was going 'all dressed up,' she quickly rhymed off excuses.

She was either going to a meeting, dance or a meal with the girls.

One balmy summer's evening, James booked a table for two in an award-winning steak house restaurant. For this date, Margaret put on her favourite tomato red Karen Millen dress and three-inch-high heeled black sandals.

"Maybe I shouldn't wear these sandals," she pondered. They were two inches higher than she usually wore. However, she concluded that the sandals perfectly matched her dress so she decided to wear them.

Margaret and James left the car in the large car park towards the rear of the restaurant. Linking hands, they strolled slowly through the streets of the market town enjoying the warmth of the sun before making their way to the steak house.

Many happy hours passed as they dined and made exciting plans for their summer together.

"Will you come with me to Marbella for a few days, Margaret?" he asked, looking into her apple green eyes.

"I would love to, James," she replied immediately.

Margaret felt there was something destined about the weekend, a weekend she would likely never forget.

Later that night, on arrival to the gate of the car park, they were stopped in their tracks. The gate was locked.

"Not to worry, James, I'm a farmer's daughter. I've climbed many a gate in my time," she assured him.

She crossed both legs over the gate and jumped to the ground. An immediate pain shot through her right foot. She screamed. She tried to hold back the tears as James jumped over the gate immediately to put his strong arms tightly around her to give her support.

"I can't put my foot to the ground," she announced in a shaky voice.

He quickly replied,

"You'll be fine, Margaret. I'll drive the car up as far as I can to the gate."

"I should never have worn these stupid sandals," Margaret cursed, holding on the rusty aluminium gate for support.

Within minutes, James had returned to her. He carried her to his car, holding her close to his broad chest. In the car, she had a closer look at her foot. She noticed a black bruise, a bruise that had stretched to her knee by the time she had arrived home.

"As soon as you get into the kitchen, put your foot into a

cold basin of water to bring down the swelling, Margaret," advised James before she opened the car door.

She knew no basin of water would solve this problem.

"If you need to go to hospital, I'm here to bring you," he promised.

Margaret stubbornly refused to go to the hospital the following day. She was pestered with questions by her family as they observed her mysterious limp. That night, she admitted to James that she needed to go to the Accident and Emergency Department.

A dreaded thought entered her mind during the stressful journey to the hospital.

"I wonder, will I need an operation?"

Margaret had never been in hospital before in her life, not to mention an operation. She breathed a sigh of relief when the radiographer stated, "You have a chipped a bone in your foot. We will put you in Plaster Paris and call you back in four weeks to see has it set."

As they left the hospital with Margaret now dressed in Plaster Paris, James announced, "You must be starving, let's go to the local hotel for lunch."

She was definitely ready to tell everyone about James. She knew that weekend that she had found her Mr. Right.

In the hotel foyer, she received a phone call. It was a call from her sister.

"Are you coming over for dinner, Margaret?" She asked.

"No," replied Margaret abruptly.

"'How do you mean no?" she questioned crossly.

"I am having dinner today with a man!" she replied swiftly.

"What man?" her sister asked.

"A special man," and followed it by a quick good bye to her sister before a thousand questions were asked. She would announce her fantastic news to her family later that evening.

Margaret wished to spend as much time as possible with James on that magical Monday. She was so happy and appreciative that this man had devoted so much of his time to her over this weekend.

This was the start of many weekends together. That August bank holiday weekend, as planned, they flew to Marbella. And that same August weekend a year later, Margaret and James became husband and wife.

'Don't Worry about a Thing'

Maria Gillooly and her husband Tim hold each other tightly and kiss outside the main entrance to the hospital. He does not accompany her any further. He is not allowed to, due to covid 19 restrictions. She tells him not to worry about a thing, assuring him that she will see him tomorrow.

"Don't forget to text me before you go to theatre," he reminds her. His eyes are showing a shade of apprehension.

"Well, that is a promise, love," she answers.

Maria carefully puts on her surgical face mask and heads towards the admissions office. She collects her medical file and is informed to head up to the fourth floor. She struts off in the direction of the lift, pulling her black wheelie bag behind her as if she was heading for a Ryanair flight. She isn't nervous. She is relieved, in fact, because she is going to have a procedure at last that should make the horrible symptoms of the past two years disappear.

Alone in the hospital lift, she becomes conscious of her

figure. She stares at herself in its aluminium mirror. She is no longer a shapely size 12 due to the continuous swallowing of steroids. Her pale face and black circles under her eyes are the result of too many sleepless nights caused by wheezing.

Maria is brought back quickly to the present as the lift slides opens. She spots the sign for St. Michael's ward and swiftly follows it until she reaches the nurse's station. A nurse is having a serious conversation on the phone. She waits. Another nurse approaches her.

"Can I help you?" she asks.

"Hello nurse, I'm Maria Gillooly. I'm booked in for a procedure and there's a bed booked for my overnight stay."

"Oh yes indeed, we were expecting you, but your bed isn't ready so just pop into this little office for a while. A member of your consultant's team shall be with you soon."

Maria steps inside, pulling her overnight bag behind her. She takes a quick look around her. She spots the familiar heart tracing machine as she calls it. She expects to have the wires of the machine stuck to her chest and stomach at some stage. Just then, a firm knock comes to the door and a young, masked female wearing a stethoscope enters.

"I'm Catherine, part of your consultant's team, Maria. I'm here to get a brief history of your complaint," she states.

"Not again," she feels like saying, for she has lost count of the number of times she has told her story to different doctors and consultants over the past couple of years. However, she cannot be rude.

"Well, I could write a book at this stage," she admits and begins to pour out her long saga while the medical student takes down some brief notes. She then informs Maria that another member of the team shall arrive shortly to speak to her.

The second intern as he describes himself, explains that he is going to carry out an ECG on her and as predicted he begins the embarrassing process of attaching the wires across her almost naked chest and stomach. Then he weighs her and then tells her he's not finished yet. He asks her to list all illnesses in her family. She calls them out and he writes them down.

"Nobody has my complaint though," she admits.

"I have another question for you, can you tell me what you are allergic to, Maria?"

"I'm only allergic to dust," she states.

"No, Maria, I mean allergies to medication."

"Ok, well, let me think. Aspirin…Tramadol…Azithromycin… and Clarithromycin. I think that's all."

'Thanks Maria," he replies and informs her as leaves the office that Dr. Treacy will be in next with the consent form.

'I feel like a guinea pig' she says to herself as she waits.

Dr. Treacy opens the door, showing off a cheery smile that would put any patient at ease.

"Maria, before I get you to sign the consent form, I want to explain first, the procedure to you and the risks involved."

"It's called in short a FESS."

"A FESS," she repeats.

"Yes, Functional Endoscopic Sinus Surgery."

'Can he not just say removal of nasal polyps?' she thinks to herself again.

He begins to list off the risks. "Bleeding, infection of the septum, brain fluid leak, visual problems…"

"Sorry to interrupt you now, doctor. I don't mean to be smart, but I'm going ahead with this procedure. I don't care what the risks are," she states.

"Well, Maria, it's protocol. We are obliged to let patients know what may go wrong."

"Ok," she replies.

"Have you any more questions for me?" he asks.

"Just one. How long have I to wait to be called down to theatre?"

"Well, hopefully you will be called within the next hour," he replies.

"If you don't have any more questions, I'd like you to sign your name just here please."

Maria willingly signs her name. The doctor exits the office clutching her file under his arm.

'Surely my bed is ready now,' she whispers to herself, opening the office door hoping to find a nurse to speak to. A nurse is standing in front of her, holding a blue and white cotton gown plus white stockings.

"You are next on the list, Maria! Will you put these on quickly and I will bring you down to pre theatre?"

The nurse begins to walk away when Maria asks her, "Put them on where, nurse? sure I don't have a bed yet."

"Oh sorry, your bed is ready, it's the one to the left of this office," she replies pointing in the appropriate direction.

She is delighted to have the room to herself while she puts on the blue and white cotton gown. She manages to tie the strings at the back of her neck and around her lower back with difficulty. Sitting on the side of the bed she groans as she pulls up the stiff tight stockings that stretches up to her thighs. She quickly covers the scanty outfit with her Marks and Spencer's fluffy pink dressing gown and slips on her cream slippers. Finally, she puts on her face mask.

The nurse returns a few minutes later and says, "It's time to go Maria."

"Hold on there, nurse, I promised I'd text my husband before I went to theatre."

The nurse shoots her eyes up to heaven.

"Tim love, I'm off to theatre. Say a little prayer for me. Talk later xx," she texts and hides the mobile phone in the bottom of her overnight bag.

In pre-theatre, she is asked to lie on a trolley by a male dressed in green scrubs. He places a red netted cap on her head informing her that the cap is as a warning to all theatre staff that she is allergic to certain medication. He then takes what looks like a plastic covered wire band and places it around Maria's upper left arm.

"This band will help to rise a vein to the surface in your arm. And before we take you down to theatre, can you tell me your name and date of birth please?" he continues.

"Why? sure, I've already told three of the team that information," she replies.

"We have to, it's hospital policy. We must make sure that we are operating on the correct person."

For the fun of it, she calls out, "Sally O' Brien, the sixth of the sixth, nineteen sixty."

"Pardon?" he says.

The expression on his face is enough.

"I'm only joking," she says and quickly gives him her correct name and date of birth. The band is very tight and uncomfortable, but she says nothing. The porter arrives and wheels her down to theatre number three and then he asks her to slide herself over on to the theatre table.

"Gosh, this table reminds me of an ironing board it's so narrow. I hope I don't fall off," she comments to the two female theatre nurses who are smiling down on her. One of them with an American accent places a heated blanket over her. The other loosens the upper tie at the back of her gown.

Maria begins to listen to lively music from the 1970s that is playing in the theatre while the male who has placed the tight band around her left upper arm taps on her bulging vein. He hasn't said he is the anaesthetist. She presumes he is. She continues to focus on the music as he inserts the cannula into her vein. She feels a sharp sting but tolerates it.

"I'm afraid I will have to take it out again," he announces within seconds but doesn't explain why.

She is the patient and believes he knows what he is doing, so she doesn't question him. He decides to tie the tight band around her other arm. This time he asks her to make a fist while he presses on the vein in the crease of her right elbow. Maria does what she is told.

"Relax your hand now," he orders and inserts the cannula once again into another bulging vein.

Maria immediately screeches. "Ah you're hurting me, stop, take it out."

He looks down at her with frustrated eyes and comments, "Well, I have never come across such a nervous patient in theatre."

"Nervous," she repeats. "You have tried twice now and you still haven't got it in," she blurts out.

"Do you want me to try the vein in the back of your hand or would you like me to get someone else?" he asks her.

"Are you qualified at all? "she mumbles under her breath.

"Excuse me?" he states.

"Oh nothing," she replies and immediately asks, "Can you please give me gas and air first?"

"That's not the way we do things around here," he answers.

Bob Marley's song 'Three little Birds' has just started playing on the radio.

She needs a distraction, and this is brilliant one.

"Don't worry about a thing, cause every little thing, is goin' to be alright!"

Just then, the theatre room doors fly open. A male, dressed in blue scrubs approaches her on the table and says in a confident and competent tone, "I'm Luke, your anaesthetist. Now, Maria, taking her left hand in his Where do you come from? And what should you be doing today?" he questions her with interest.

Maria is so busy answering his questions she does not realise the cannula is inserted. Maria's suspicion is correct. The other guy is not qualified at all.

"Don't worry about a thing, Maria, you just relax and slowly inhale gas and air through this mask," Luke tells her.

Within seconds, Maria feels as if she had just knocked back a couple of gin and tonics.

The next voice she hears is the sound of a female voice calling out, "Maria, you are in recovery now, can you hear me?"

Maria takes a while to open her heavy-laden eyes to see who is speaking.

"How are you?" a female nurse asks softly.

"I am alive, thank god," Maria replies.

With eyes now open, she tells the nurse she has a pounding pain in her nose.

"That is only natural," the nurse says and gives Maria some pain-relieving medication to swallow.

Her consultant arrives to her bedside. In her usual calm soft tone, she says, "You gave me a hard time."

"A hard time?" Maria whispers.

"Yes, you had quite a few nasal polyps to be removed so the procedure took longer than usual, however I have successfully removed them all."

Maria cannot wait to get back to the ward to ring her darling Tim to tell him the wonderful news. And she will sing to him too. She will sing,

"Don't worry about a thing 'cause every little thing is goin' be alright!" …

‘Kitchen Floor Conflict’

It happens every Saturday morning. As soon as breakfast is over, he begins his weekend morning ritual. He insists on opening wide, the four kitchen windows. It doesn’t matter whether there’s a beastly wind blowing outside or the rain is racing down the window pain. The job must be done. And it must be done by him. She has suggested many times that she, his wife will do it at a time that suits her but he always turns down the offer.

“This is my chore. You don’t have the elbow grease to do the job. You need to put your back into it,” he tells her.

Still dressed in her winter white dressing gown, she watches him with frustration, grinding the sponge head of the floor mop onto the beige square tiles. She believes some day he will lift a tile off the floor or crack the plastic mop head from the pressure he uses as he pushes the mop over and back. She offers to help him move the kitchen table and chairs in order to wash the floor properly.

“There is no need to move anything,” he swiftly replies.

And then she informs him, “There is no need to open all the

windows either, sure if you use boiling water, the floor will dry in minutes."

He does not like been watched. "Have YOU nothing to do?" and begins to list of things she can do while he takes a break for a few seconds holding tightly on the mop.

"Why don't you go into the sitting room and watch some morning TV or read another chapter from your library book?" he suggests.

No further suggestions or offers are made. She enters the sitting room. He continues to mop. By doing so there is no further kitchen floor conflict.

'Out of the Top Drawer'

All the excitement began on the evening of her twin son's arts ball. Nell was happily trying to keep in tune as she sang along to Nathan Carter's song, 'Wagon wheel' as it blared away on the radio. She was carefully ironing her son's new white shirt at the same time. Her retired husband sat in his kitchen fireside chair trying to read the front-page news of the local newspaper when he looked up at his wife and spoke.

"Do you not think it would be better if you focused on your ironing instead?" he suggested.

"Now why would I stop singing, Denis, today above all days?" she smiled.

Denis was teasing his dear wife of twenty-five years knowing she was in mighty form. It was no doubt a proud evening for both of them. She was doing her best to help their sons get ready for their 'big night'. Well, one of them, Simon actually. Her other son, Greg was still 'the same two and four pence,' as she described him. He had no interest in clothes at all. He would quite happily wear the same shirt and trousers to every function he attended. Greg definitely took after her husband. Denis wouldn't have a stitch of clothes to wear if it wasn't for his fashion-conscious wife. She always made sure that he looked his best for all occasions. Nell held up the new shirt she purchased for Simon and asked Denis to tell him what he thought of it.

"It's alright I suppose," came his quick answer.

Nell emphasized that it was a Peter England shirt and showing his ignorance, he replied "Who's he?"

"The designer of the shirt," she laughed while taking clothes out of the laundry basket. She had also purchased a new tie, socks and new boxer shorts for Simon.

Denis stared at his wife in shock and eventually managed to say to her.

"Please tell me that you are not buying him his underwear too."

She had bought the boxers on purpose for she knew Denis was very conservative and continued with her teasing.

"Sure, who will see them, only himself," swaying the boxer shorts in the air. In the process, she hit her finger off the hot iron and let out a shout,

"Now look what you made me do, Denis," and ran to the kitchen sink to place her finger under the cold running tap.

There was an uneasy silence in the kitchen. Denis felt sorry for upsetting his wife. He was well aware that she was a fun-loving, caring wife and mother.

Denis broke the silence by asking her where had their two sons disappeared to. She informed him that Simon was still in the shower and Greg was still stuck in front of the television with not a sign of lifting himself from the leather couch to get ready for the happy event.

No sooner had she made these statements, when smart looking Simon arrived into the kitchen wearing a brand-new suit.

Greg followed, dressed in Levi's jeans, navy stripped Tee-shirt and the black leather jacket that he has been wearing for donkey's years.

Nell couldn't believe that Simon was dressed already and noticed he was wearing a brand-new suit.

"I'm running late," he stated quickly.

"Late…"…"Late," she repeated. "But the ball isn't starting for another two hours, Simon."

Simon was getting red in the face as he began to give a brief explanation that he had places to go and things to do. Greg laughed at his brother excuses. His mother wondered what was so funny. She was not impressed at all by Greg's poor effort to dress up for his arts ball.

"I take it that you are ready to go too,"

"I sure am," Greg answered.

"Are you not going to wear this lovely new shirt that I bought especially for you, Simon?" pointing to the Peter England shirt that lay on the back of the kitchen chair.

The expression on Simon's face was enough but unwilling to hurt his mother's feelings, he promised to wear the shirt on some other occasion. Nell had also gone to the bother of getting his navy single breasted suit dry cleaned. Nell made the mad suggestion to Greg that he could wear his twin brother's suit to the ball instead. Greg burst out laughing.

"It's not my wedding day. Will you calm down, mother?"

Ignoring his comments, Nell turned her attention to Simon's fancy suit and wished to know where he purchased it. On hearing the news that he bought it in Brown Thomas, she was anxious to know how much he paid for it. When she heard that he paid 500 euro for it, she was totally shocked and wondered how he managed to save for it and he just graduating from college.

"But it was reduced to 200 euro in the sale," Simon added.

Suddenly, her mind was diverted to her own wedding day. She reminded Denis of how handsome he looked, dressed in his French navy pinstriped suit.

"Am I not still handsome, Nell?" he piped up.

"Of course, you are love, you are out of the top drawer."

Greg interrupted. "Mum, can you put on a fry for me, I might not get a bite later."

"And what about me, mother? Do I not look handsome too?" interrupted Simon.

"Not only are you handsome you, too, are out of the top-drawer Simon."

"What does that even mean, mother?"

"It means that you're one of the best sons that any mother could wish for."

"Mother, what about my fry?" Greg said, interrupting her once again. Then, Simon informed all that he had to leave immediately.

Nell's only interest at that moment was to convince Greg to wear a shirt and tie to the ball, hinting that formal wear might help him attract a girlfriend. Her suggestion was ignored, so for the fun of it, she rushed to the laundry basket and picked up the boxer shorts.

"Would you like try these on for size?" trying to keep a straight face. He ignored her again.

"Ok so, you, my son can on put your own fry since you are in no rush to go the arts ball."

"Where are the rashers and sausages?" Greg sulked.

"Well, they're not to be found in the laundry basket, she laughed, and then directed her husband to the task of setting the table. Suddenly, she heard a familiar voice.

"Greg"..."Greg."

Simon had returned to the kitchen again. He grabbed Greg by the arm and pulled him towards the back kitchen door while he explained that his banger of a car would not start.

"I am going to have to take your car, dad, and Greg, you will have to come now if you want a lift. My girlfriend will think I stood her up," he added.

"What about my fry?" cried Greg.

"Girlfriend! You have a girlfriend!" said Nell, delighted to hear Simon's surprising news.

"My car," cried Denis.

"You mean our car, Denis."

"Of course, you can have it, love."

Denis had Nell all to himself that evening. And that evening he realised that he was blessed with a fantastic wife and two fine sons. It was now his turn to tell Nell that she too was indeed "out of the top drawer."

'She Didn't Come Here for a Haircut'

Anne was nervous about her medical procedure. She expected her husband to leave early the following morning to bring her to the hospital, a ninety-minute journey away. However, she did not expect the answer she got from him.

"Sure, can't you get the bus to the hospital. I'll collect you later," he said casually.

"Get the bus?" she repeated, not believing what he had just said.

"Yes, why not? I have a day's work to do."

Her voice grew louder. "So, you are telling me that your work is more important than your wife's health."

"No, but it would be handy if you..."

Anne interrupted, "Handy?" "Handy?" You are your own boss; you can bring your laptop with you and carry out your business in the car. If you get bored, you can go for a walk or visit a church to say a prayer for me." Anne had been through a similar procedure before. She would fast for many hours, have endless repetitive medical questions hurled at her and she dreaded the insertion of a cannula before being put to sleep.

After a long silence, he said, "Ok, I will bring you, but you know how I feel about hospitals."

Next day, they arrived early to the hospital car park. Oliver offered to buy her a coffee and muffin in the local Supermac's to pass the time.

"I'm fasting, Oliver," she reminded him. Instead, they sat in the car listening to Classic hits FM until it was time to go to the main entrance, the location of the admittance office. She informed him that there was no need for him to go to the ward with her. She promised to ring to let him know the time she would be discharged. He planted a tender kiss on her lips and wished her the best of luck.

"See you later, my queen."

A content smile filled her face as she waved him goodbye.

Oliver arrived to the day ward earlier than planned. Anne was sitting on the hospital chair, still dressed in the hospital gown, still fasting and still waiting for the cannula to be removed.

"Are you not dressed yet?" he asked her.

"No, love, I got delayed getting back from the recovery room."

He looked at his watch. Anne recognised the cause of his irritation: She knew he was hungry. He always got irritable when he was hungry.

The nurse looking after Anne was seated in the corner of the day ward writing up her notes and was obviously eaves dropping in on their conversation. Suddenly, she sprung from her swinging chair and took her stand beside Oliver.

"Excuse me, sir, your wife has just been through a general anaesthetic. She didn't come here for a haircut. She has had nothing to eat. The cannula is still inserted, and she needs her medical prescription." She suggested that Oliver treat himself to some refreshments in the hospital cafe and would welcome him back at 6 pm. Her tone was polite but firm. Oliver made no attempt to question or answer the nurse.

Anne was secretly enjoying the drama unfolding in front of her, especially the expression of embarrassment on her husband's face.

"I will see you at six so, Anne," he stated while his wife managed to keep a serious face.

"See you at six, Oliver."

By 6pm, Anne had got dressed. She had devoured the tea and toast. The cannula was gone and she was now waiting for her prescription. And Oliver was back.

"Thank God you are ready. Come on, I'll carry your bag."

He gave Anne no chance to speak. A familiar voice from behind him spoke to him instead. He turned around briskly to listen to the same nurse explain another house rule.

"You cannot walk her to the hospital entrance, Mr Fallon! Anne will be brought to the front door of the hospital in a wheelchair! It is hospital policy."

Just then, the doctor on duty interrupted the conversation to present Anne with her prescription. Oliver left the ward. He returned, rearing to go with a wheelchair for Anne.

"Sit in quick." His voice was rushed. The nurse shook her head.

"YOU cannot push your wife in the wheelchair. That is the job of the porter." Oliver took a deep breath and stayed silent. He sighed with relief when the porter arrived.

He stayed silent until he got Anne safely into the car.

"I never want to see that nurse again, or this hospital either." His frustration continued. "Anne, I've waited around all day to collect you and now I'm being treated like a…a schoolboy."

"She was only following hospital procedures, Oliver. And, you know something else, love?" An instant smirk stretched across her face.

“What?” he replied, looking bewildered.

She beckoned him to move closer. “I didn’t come here for a haircut.”

They both burst into an uncontrollable laughter.

He drove ‘his queen’ to her favourite hotel on the way home for dinner. Their laughter and the taste of delicious food had freed them from the stress of the day.

'To Appraise or Not to Appraise'

Dedicated to Trish Barrett and Aisling Macken

Roger stood in front of the oval mirror that hung on the wall of his small principal's office fixing his navy and white blue pinstriped tie while singing along to the Dolly Parton's hit song 'Nine to Five'. He was about to conduct an appraisal on one of his teachers. He took a look at his Fitbit. 'She's running late,' he said to himself.

A firm knock came to his office door. It must be her, he thought. He opened it slowly.

"Sorry, Roger, I know I'm a half an hour late but I can explain. You see one of the parents rang me and I just couldn't get her off the phone."

"Not to worry, Trish, these things happen. Take a seat." Trish spotted a bowl of Scots clan sweets sitting in a circular bowl on a small coffee table.

"Would you mind if I had one of your sweets first?"

"Sure, go on," he replied with a chuckle.

Trish unfolded the sweet paper and sat on the black two-seater leather couch in the corner of the office facing the rectangular coffee table.

"Ah, Trish, if you don't mind, I would prefer if you could sit in this chair as this is a formal appraisal not a discussion."

"Sure, no problem," and she grabbed another sweet from the crystal bowl before sitting down in front of the principal's cluttered desk. Rather than eat the second sweet, she slipped it into her handbag and decided it was better not to ask her principal if he would like one himself.

"Now Trish, I would like to explain the appraisal to you. The purpose of it is to help find out your strengths and weaknesses and show you how to develop your potential in future teaching jobs."

"Really?" she replied in a surprised tone.

"I will begin by asking you what you think went well for you in your teaching during the past year?"

"Absolutely everything, Roger, sure, you see my classroom on a daily basis. You know that I am very motivated, enthusiastic, artistic and always willing to take on a challenge. And the taking on of the confirmation class was definitely a challenge. I never prepared for one of those before."

"You are an assertive and confident lady alright; I must admit," answered Roger.

He continued with the questions, looking down at a sheet of paper on his desk to remind himself of his next question. After clearing his throat, he asked her.

"What would you do differently in your next job?"

"Absolutely nothing. As the saying goes 'If it ain't broke, don't fix it'."

"Absolutely nothing?" he repeated. "Do you not think there is always room for improvement Trish?"

"Well as far as I am concerned, one can only do their best. And I do that," she replied in a serious tone.

Roger let out a deep sigh. "Right," he said and took a long pause before asking the next question. "Could you suggest to me ways that you could be more obliging to your colleagues?"

"Obliging," she repeated. "Why? Are you suggesting that there are colleagues who are saying I am not."

"Of course not, Trish."

A frustrated look crept across Trish's face.

"Then why are you asking me all these questions for? I don't mean to be rude but if it's supposed to be an appraisal, well, I haven't received much praise or positive feedback yet."

Keeping a straight face, he continued with his questioning. "Have you any suggestions as to how we could make things easier for you and teachers in general?"

"Well, for starters, the school day starts far too early. I'm exhausted getting up every morning after hours of preparation work and corrections the night before. When I was going to school, teachers had a great time. They didn't start teaching till 9:25am and they got a fifty-five-minute lunch break. There's no time to relax now at all and there's too much paperwork," she informed him in an agitated tone.

"It is a long time ago since you were in school, Trish!"

Trish stared at him. She had had enough of his intimidating questions. "Yes, Roger, it is a long time since I was in school. And I've acquired many qualifications, achievements and hobbies since which I am very proud of."

"Very interesting Trish," came his short reply.

Trish couldn't believe what she was hearing. 'What is the purpose of this so-called appraisal' she thought to herself.

"I have one more question for you. What is your goal for the coming year?"

"I'm going to take "one day at a time" as the song goes. You should remember it, it's about forty years old now," she replied in a sarcastic tone.

"Yes, I think I might have heard it. Does it go like this? *"I'm only human, I'm just a woman, help me believe…"*

He was unable to continue as he burst out laughing.

"What's going on," she asked him.

"I'm sorry Trish but this has been a mock appraisal. We don't do appraisals on teachers when they are leaving a school however, I do have one big surprise for you."

A big smile then beamed across her face.

"A surprise for me," she repeated with great excitement in her voice.

"Yes, your qualifications, your creative teaching and your personality has stood out over the past year with us, your colleagues and parents of all the children in your class. The staff and parents do agree that you have given one hundred and ten percent to your teaching and so I'd like to present you with a cheque as a result of money collected for you by your school colleagues, parents and the Board of Management."

"Oh thank you, that is so kind of you all, thank you, thank you" and she went to hug the principal.

"Take is easy now, Trish," he said to the embarrassed teacher.

He placed the cheque in her hand and wished her the best of luck in her new job. Trish had got what she wanted, praise and appreciation for a job well done.

'There IS a Reason'

Dedicated to Orla Faragher, reunited after 12 years.

Sometimes people come into our lives for a short period, never to meet again. Sometimes they stay with us for life. Some leave us and are destined to return at some stage. Orla and Josephine came into each other lives in 1999 as work colleagues. Three years later, new careers for both of them caused them to go their separate ways. Orla and her young family moved to Co. Kildare while Josephine started her teaching career in Co. Roscommon. Unfortunately, they did not keep up contact. Josephine was always hopeful that they would rekindle their relationship someday. For twelve years, Josephine, paid a few visits to their former work place hoping some member of staff would have heard from her. The answer was 'no' every time. Orla and Josephine shared a common bond. Both of them had a deep love for their elderly parents. Both were blessed with a deep faith and were full of fun and mischief. They believed that events in life happened for a reason.

In June 2014, just days before the celebration of both their birthdays, Orla's maiden name flashed across her mind like a banner. "Gavin, Gavin, that's it." She had remembered it at last. She also remembered the town in Mayo where she grew up. Josephine found the number in the phone book and excitedly rang it hoping that someone in the family home would answer. Orla's dear dad answered and he was only too delighted to share Orla's mobile number with a good friend and colleague of old.

That evening, Josephine made the long-waited phone call to her. Orla was thrilled to hear the familiar voice and thought what a wonderful surprise for her birthday. During that phone call they agreed on the location for their re-union; Kildare Village, as they both had a love for clothes shopping.

Josephine made an effort to look her best for the re-union. Wearing her three-quarter length multi-coloured floral dress from Zara, her pink suede two-inch heels and her newly cut bobbed hairstyle that showed off her silver-streaked hair. She was ready for the meeting. She was sure that she had left plenty of time to reach the bus stop. The summer sun kissed her sallow face as she strolled along the side path to catch the local bus into the city before boarding the M7. Suddenly, the No. 122 whizzed by and pulled up at the bus stop. Josephine tried to walk a little faster to catch the bus before it departed. But no, her high heels prevented her from reaching the bus stop in time. The bus took off.

"There is a reason I have missed it," she stated with confidence. She did not panic even though she was aware that she may now miss the M7 bus to Kildare Village to meet her long lost friend at the specified time. She continued to walk into the city. Sauntering along the side path, a male, with a Dublin accent grabbed her attention from behind. He was speaking loudly on his mobile phone. Josephine could not help eavesdropping in on his conversation.

"I've lost my bank card. And I have searched the shops and restaurant I visited but no one has found it. I went to the bus station but the bus driver would not let me on the bus without full payment. I am only six euro short," the voice said.

Josephine immediately turned around and addressed the tall casually dressed concerned male.

"Excuse me," she said, interrupting his phone conversation, "I have been listening to your unfortunate situation. I will give you the six euro for the bus fare," she said smiling at him. The man's eyes and mouth opened wide on hearing the news and immediately informed the person on the phone that he had to go. Josephine counted out the six euros coins that she had in her dress pocket and placed them in the man's right hand.

"Just see me as your guardian angel," she told him. He smiled broadly and thanked her courteously. He informed her that he was on his way home to Mullingar. She wished him a safe journey and waved him goodbye.

"Yes, I was right, I knew there was a reason why I missed that bus."

Josephine was delighted that she was able to help out someone who was in need. Now, she turned her attention to her friend Orla. She was hopeful that she may catch the M7 Express in time. She landed into the city with just enough time to hop on the bus. Her kindness had brought her luck. She was on her way at last to Kildare Village to meet her long lost friend.

Orla was waiting eagerly to meet Josephine at Kildare Village bus stop. They hugged each other tight.

"You've haven't changed a bit, Orla Gavin" Josephine announced.

"Well, I have to say the same to yourself. You're still as young looking as ever."

They both admitted that they were starving so they decided

to head towards the nearest restaurant. Thankfully, there wasn't a long queue and they were shown to the seats immediately.

That summer afternoon, they spent hours recalling their fun times working together all those years ago and Orla was dying to know about Josephine love life as she been slagging her for so long about finding a husband. Their coffee cups were continually refilled as the conversations on various topics continued. Orla took special interest in the incident that happened to her friend earlier that day.

"Sure, Josephine you were always a kind-hearted person, putting yourself last and giving your time to other people. And you were always a fantastic woman to organize a party, might I add."

"Well, Orla, you have similar qualities yourself and that is why I was eager to meet up with you once again."

It was like they had never parted company. They spent so much time chatting that they had forgotten the time.

"O no, Orla, look at the time, we have left no time to go clothes shopping."

"Don't you worry, girl; this is the first of many visits for you to Kildare Village. On your next visit, we will shop 'till we drop', so bring the credit card with you," joked Orla.

Before Josephine got back on the M7 bus that evening, Orla handed her a white envelope. "What is in the envelope?" she asked with curiosity.

"Open it." Josephine opened it slowly. It contained a 'Paddy Powers' betting ticket, displaying two numbers, 7, and 11, the dates of both their birthdays. "I hope they turn up in tonight's main lotto." stated Orla.

Later that night, Josephine phoned Orla. "Orla, guess what? The two numbers have come up in the lotto."

"I know, and I am delighted but not a bit surprised. You deserve a win after your good deed today. In fact, I am more delighted that we are reunited after all these years. And you know there IS a reason why we found each other again, just you wait and see." Josephine added.

Thought you had Forgotten

Dedicated to Simon and Marette Kennedy

A broad secret smile stretched across her youthful face as she heard the back kitchen door open. It was her newly married husband of just six months. He had been playing a club hurling match that evening. She quickly tightened the belt of her baby pink dressing gown she had recently purchased. She raced to the brown leather couch and stretched her long-tanned legs over the length of it. The tulip red nail varnished toes peeped out through the top of her open slippers.

"Marette, where are you, love?" She heard him call.

"In the living room, Simon," she replied swiftly as she turned on the television.

He raced in to tell her the exciting news that his team had won the hurling match easily. Marette, who didn't have much interest in the game replied,

"Will you calm down, Simon, you'd swear you never won a

match before," and began tapping the couch, prompting him to come over and sit down beside her. She had planned to spoil him with his favourite sandwich: chicken salad and a cup of Barry's tea. She always had a special treat ready for him when he came home after a match. Simon suddenly took a long look at Marette. He was puzzled.

"Why are you wearing your dressing gown at this hour of the evening?"

"I thought we would have a cosy night in and watch the 'Late Late Show' later on," she stated in her usually cheery tone.

"The Late Late Show?" he repeated.

"Yes," she replied quickly as she could not wait to report to him about one of the special guests on the show.

"Nathan Carter, your favourite singer is on tonight's show and he's singing 'Wagon Wheel,' she said excitedly.

Simon was not impressed by his wife's decision, and he was now feeling the hunger pangs.

"Will you make me an ould sandwich Marette, please, with a nice cup of tea? I'm starving."

As she was leaving the living room to enter the kitchen, he called after her, "And can you bring me a slice of that sponge cake you made yesterday."

Turning her head back immediately, she responded, "No, I'm sorry, it's Lent, Simon. Sure, you know that you are on a special diet while you are playing those hurling matches. And just to let you know, I made that sponge cake for my mother," she added.

Simon was getting more confused and began to ask his wife a few questions. "Marette, were you in Eason's book shop during the week?"

Without blinking an eye, she replied, "I was. I've all the St. Patrick's day cards bought and sent if that is what you're wondering about. I'd be waiting a long time for you to get that job done," she laughed.

"And did you buy any other type of card?" he continued.

"Ah…Yes, I bought…ah...Easter cards while I was there but it's a bit too soon to send them out, don't you think? Now I better go and get you that sandwich, Simon," she announced quickly to avoid further questioning.

"Hold on a minute, I've something to tell you. I was in Shaws yesterday having a look at the new spring collection of shirts that has just arrived in and I was admiring…"

Marette quickly cut in on his sentence. "What were you doing in Shaws?"

"Sure, didn't I buy you two new shirts for Christmas?" she stated. "What are you looking for another shirt for? Will you stop, you could set up a second-hand shop at this stage. You have far too many of them in every colour one could think of, tightly pack into that wardrobe of yours," she continued.

As she looked closely at her husband's face, she could see his frustrated look had changed to one of anger as he sprung from the couch to walk over to her.

"Now will you tell me this much, are we going out tonight or what?" he asked her loudly.

"Going out?" she repeated. "Sure, Simon, pet, we go out nearly every weekend, and what are all the questions for? Is it a St. Patrick's Day quiz or what?" she teased.

"No, Marette, it's not a St. Patrick's Day quiz" however, I have ONE more question for you?" His voice was getting louder.

"What question is that?" she asked gently.

"What date is it today?"

Marette, trying to keep her composure and trying her best not to laugh, answered "The sixteenth of March." And then began to open slowly the baby pink dressing gown to reveal a Ted baker Forest green jersey dress. She had bought it just the day before especially for the occasion. She flung off her dressing gown and threw her arms around her dear husband, hugging him tightly and wished him a happy birthday. A glowing smile crept back into Simon face. His playful wife hadn't forgotten his birthday after all.

"O Marette, love, I thought you had forgotten my birthday," and kissed her tenderly on the lips.

"How could I forget your birthday, darlin?" she stated.

"Do you know what, Marette? You'd make a fine actress! There is no doubt about it."

"Well, you know what, Simon, I might just do that, for the local drama club are looking for new members for their upcoming new stage comedy."

"Well, I think that is a great idea. When I'm at hurling practice, you can be at drama practice. Now come here to me and I'll sing you a verse of 'Wagon Wheel'."

"O, we will have plenty of time for that later on, Simon."

She walked around to the back of the cream leather couch and bending down, she picked up a colourful bag with happy birthday written on it. "Go and try that on quickly. I have booked dinner for 8pm for the two of us in your favourite Chinese restaurant."

"You were in Shaws after all," he laughed, as he ran up the stairs to change.

"Of course, love," she replied, making her way eventually towards the kitchen to light the birthday candles on the blue and yellow iced cake and to set the Nathan Carter CD ready to play his favourite song.

'Valentine Shocks'

The attentive and mannerly waiter pulls out the mahogany and leather covered chairs for the handsome couple. He then places paper napkins over their knees, hands them both the menu booklet and leaves them to choose from the set or A La carte menu. Charlie takes a long look at his girlfriend's face. He doesn't like her expression. He feels there is something just not right.

"What's wrong, Carmel, don't you like the restaurant?" he asks her.

"Well, Charlie, I thought you'd bring me to a fancy restaurant; after all, it is our first Valentines night together since we got engaged. You know, like EPNS silver cutlery, white linen tablecloth, a rose on the table. The menu is boring and there's very little choice to select from," she continues while staring at the menu.

Charlie is surprised by her reaction. He brought her here on their first date and he was sure it would be the ideal place to return to. After all, it was here where their romance first blossomed.

"A now come on, Carmel, we have to save up, it's only six months to our wedding," he found himself saying.

Carmel replied with a sigh. "I suppose you're right."

Charlie looks down at the menu and suddenly Carmel's favourite dishes catch his eye. He turns the menu booklet around towards his fiancé.

"Look, Carmel, French onion soup for starters and fillet steak with garlic sauce and asparagus for mains. Sure, you love fillet steak!"

The waiter happens to pass by their table.

"Excuse me waiter," Charlie says politely.

"Yes, sir how can I help you?"

"Could you bring us your wine list please?"

The efficient waiter replies, "Of course sir, I will back in a jiffy with it."

"I've been looking forward to this date all-week Charlie, just the two of us," she admits looking into his sky-blue eyes.

Charlie's cheeks are blushing as if he is feeling guilty about something. There is indeed something that he had kept from her and now he must tell her.

"Ah, Carmel, I have…invited someone else along to join us," he says clearing his throat.

"What?…You have invited someone else. Who?" raising her voice.

"Paul," he answers immediately.

"Paul…your brother Paul?"

"Yes, Carmel, I felt sorry for him. He has no one to celebrate Valentine's night with so I thought it would be nice to invite him along."

"All the nights there are in the year, and you had to go and pick Valentine's night to bring him out to dinner."

"Well, I honestly didn't think you mind."

"Mind, of course I mind. And I was wondering too why you didn't book a table for two, but now it makes sense."

Carmel puts her two hands up to her face in frustration. She has never heard the likes of it. "Who brings their brother along with them to a Valentine dinner?" she bursts out.

Charlie looks up and spots his brother walking towards their table. He begins to panic and whispers to Carmel to take her hands down from her face as his brother is about to join them. Paul pulls out the seat beside Charlie.

"Hello, Charlie and Carmel, thanks very much for the invite. You're very thoughtful, both of you," he says with a super smile on his face.

Paul has put great effort into his outfit. He is wearing a smart navy blazer, a baby pink shirt and is even wearing a tie. Carmel has never seen him dressed up in formal wear before.

"You have always been a generous brother. I know where to go if I ever need a loan." Paul jokes.

Carmel stares at Paul and then turns her head to stare at her fiancée. What did Paul mean by that comment? She is puzzled.

"Gosh aren't you a lucky woman, Carmel!" he states.

"What do you mean by that, Paul?"

"I'm just saying that he's a very generous man in every way with his money and his time."

They are suddenly interrupted by the return of the waiter.

"Now sir, here is the wine list…And shall I bring you the menu now as our restaurant is very busy tonight?"

Paul asks the waiter if he could come back in a few minutes as he is expecting one more person to join the table. Charlie cannot help himself as he lets out a shout "one more" loud enough to attract the attention of the other customers in the restaurant.

"One more," Carmel repeats the phrase in a much louder voice.

Charlie and Carmel look at each other and then both look at Paul.

"What are you playing at Paul?" he asks his brother angrily.

Paul swiftly replies "I have something to tell you both. Please don't be angry with me, I didn't want to upset you and ruin your night but…"

"But what?" asks a frustrated Charlie.

Carmel demands an answer, telling him to go on and explain himself.

A very nervous Paul lets the 'cat out of the bag.'

"I have met a woman and I invited her along tonight so that she could get to know you both better."

Carmel can't believe what she is hearing. Paul has never been known to have dated any woman because he is so shy and awkward around them.

"A woman…a girlfriend you mean. Well, aren't you the 'dark horse'? How did you manage to keep that one quiet?" asks Charlie.

Charlie and Carmel are now eager to know who this woman is.

"You actually know her Charlie, she's a teacher in your school."

Charlie's mind begins to race as he tries to think of all the single female teachers in the school. He thinks of teachers that are around Paul's age. And a teacher that would suit Paul's personality.

It couldn't be Mary Murphy; she is four years older than him, so he starts naming out the three teachers that are around his age. Could it be quiet spoken Kate Bracken, mad Philomena O' Connor or talkative Paula Callaghan?

Paul answers a definite no to each name he calls out.

"Ah come on, I give up, who it is so?" Charlie asks.

"Mary Murphy," announces Paul with great pride.

"Mary Murphy, you're joking me," replies Charlie.

"I didn't call her out because she's too old for you," replies Charlie.

"What's four years? Sure, age doesn't matter when you have met the right person," replies Paul.

"Mary Murphy, well I thought I'd never see the day when she'd meet a fella. She such an academic. She always has her head stuck in a book," says Charlie.

Paul urgently tells them both to shush as he sees Mary approach their table. Mary is 'dressed to the nines' as always, wearing a tomato red fitted Phase Eight dress with a Swarovski crystal necklace and earrings to match. And her glossy brown hair shows off a glam curl blow-dry.

"Sorry I'm late everybody, I thought I'd never get out of the hairdressers," she announces, taking up her seat across from Paul.

"Hello Mary, this is a surprise, I didn't think I'd be seeing you until after the school mid-term break," Charlie comments.

Carmel has other thoughts running through her head and blurts out.

"A surprise Charlie? This is more like a Valentine shock and I'm just wondering how many more shocks am I going to receive before the night is over?" she states, staring across at Paul and Mary.

Charlie ignores his fiancé's comment as he does not want to create a scene. After all, he works in the same school so he must remain diplomatic. However, Charlie is eager to know more about the romance.

"Well, come on now tell us how did ye meet each other?"

"You might find it hard to believe it, but we met at a country and western dance. A fella by the name of Jimmy Buckley was playing on the night. You must know him Charlie, he had a big hit with "Your Wedding Day" and bursts into the first verse of the song.

"The first time I saw you, I loved you with all of my heart, the first time…"

"Never heard of him or the song," interrupts Carmel who is far more interested in finding out just how long this courtship has been going on.

"Oh since last July, Carmel. We met at a race dance in Roscommon."

"What? Seven months and you never said a word to me," replied Charlie.

"Yes, seven months."

Mary is fed up with all questions being hurled at her boyfriend and now wants the focus to be placed on her so she changes the subject.

"Now lads, what do you think of my new faux fur coat?" rising swiftly from her chair to model it for them. She proudly informs them that Paul bought it for her as Valentine's Day gift.

"It's lovely Mary," answers Carmel in a sarcastic tone.

Paul puts his arm around Mary's shoulder when she returns to her seat. And then tells his brother and his fiancé that he has more news for them.

"More news," repeats Charlie.

Carmel and Charlie look at each other. Carmel senses that there is another shock in store and covers her face with her hands again.

Paul calls the waiter over.

"Sir, are you ready to order now?" he asks politely.

"Yes, can you bring me your best bottle of Champagne and leave the menu for another while."

"But, sir, it's getting very late, I need to take your order now please."

Paul admits that there's no hunger on him at all.

"Champagne," repeats Charlie staring at his brother.

Paul turns to Mary and says "Do you know what I'd like to

do, Mary?"

"What's that dear?" gazing into his soft hazel brown eyes.

"I'd like to make an honest woman out of you and take you home to Roscommon."

"Are you proposing marriage to me, Paul?"

"I sure am, my lovely."

"Now how could I say no to a fabulous man with a few fine acres of land. Yes, yes, yes of course I will marry you," throwing her arms around Paul's neck.

The waiter rushes back with the Champagne and glasses and pours it into four tall glasses for them. Both couples are about to sip the alcohol when suddenly the background music is turned up.

"Listen, Paul, that's our song," Mary says excitedly.

Carmel looks at Charlie and then throws her eyes up to heaven.

Paul had it all planned earlier with the manager for the song to be played for the two of them. He begins to belt out the lyrics of Etta James's classic hit.

"At last, my love has come along
My lonely days are over
And life is like a song" ...

As soon as the song is over Carmel quickly offers to make a toast.

"Let us make a toast to no more Valentine shocks," as she clinks her glass off the three others.

"No more Valentine shocks," promises Paul with a great big grin on his face and then proceeds to make a suggestion to his generous brother.

"How about making it a double wedding brother?"

Charlie and Carmel have heard it all. It is time to make a quick getaway. But Carmel has something to say to Mary before leaving.

"You have ruined our Valentine's dinner; you're such a selfish article!"

There is an immediate reply from the sarcastic Mary. "Ah now, Carmel, you only lost out on a dinner. Look on the bright side, you're gaining a sensational sister-in-law."

Poetry Section

'A Birthday Prayer'

Dedicated to the two Galway Girls; Phil Concannon and Breda Murphy

Dear God, please, this birthday night,
I pray you'll get these few things right.
Keep those flushes far away!
Had enough, day after day.

I pray no wrinkles will never be seen.
I promise to plaster the nightly cream.
No bags under my eyes, I beg of you.
Don't let my bum sag, whatever you do.

I can hide my grey hair with henna and dye.
To keep my flat belly, on you, I'll rely.
My mood is pleasant, now keep it that way.
Tears and Tantrums must stay well at bay.

Take care of my bones! Keep them sturdy and strong!
Grant me a healthy life, make it good and long!
No frequent urges for the bathroom please.
Or accidents when I laugh or sneeze.

God, let my memory always remain,
So, there's no chance, I'll go insane.
Miracles may be needed for what I ask
That's why I chose you to take on the task.

'Birthday Party'

Dedicated to my school friends who attended the 50th birthday party

'Is this a birthday party or bankers meeting?
Just take a look at the serious seating.
Everyone takes up their places.
You never saw such happier faces.

Orders taken for red or white,
Toasts all round for a fabulous night.
Photos from school days are passed around.
Images of us all, eventually found.
Worn magazines, looked slowly through.
'Is that me?...ah, look at you!'

As we gather round to take a view, including half the town.
'Who's this?' somebody shouts. 'All I can see is black and white
'And sure, I can't see much at this time of night.'
A phone produced then a flashing light,
'Will you turn off that thing it's far too bright?'

Manuel, Manuel, will you give us the bill.
I think by now we've had our fill.
A tip for the waiter, as coins are passed,
Counting them quick, we get out fast.
Out we go, to the nearest bar,
We're fifty now, can't walk too far.

Laughter and jokes fill the air
As stories from the eighties, we joyfully share.
Photos are taken of the eventful night
Shared through Facebook, oh what a sight!
Hugs galore before we leave, no need for tears
We'll meet again, this time next year.

'You Look 29 Sweetheart'

Dedicated to Noreen & Denis Dunne

It is your birthday and
It's time to party.
For you are someone I admire and do appreciate.
You are so loving and oh so kind.
Isn't it great, having you here, as part of my life?
You look 29 Sweetheart
And not, another year more.
Just tell me what I
can do to look like you.
Not even a line or a wrinkle,
No pimples or spots to view.
Tell me your secret, show me the creams so
I can look like you.
Is it the jogging or the walking each day?
Well darling, you know I'm looking for tips so
I'll take what you give.
Your smiles and your laughter,
Your quietness and calm.
This is why I think, you look so well.
Cherish this moment, you should cherish this day,
For days like these, are precious and few.
I want you to know that
Happiness and peace, good health and luck is what
I wish for you,
from your man who loves you so.

'Covid 19 Birthday'

Dedicated to Mary Casey

Put on your broad smile, let out a loud cheer and
Forget about covid, your birthday is here.
Fill your home with flowers and balloons.
All will be admired through WhatsApp or Zoom.

Turn up the music, and sing along
'Happy Birthday To you' that well known song.
Birthday wishes from family and friends and,
Let's raise a toast to covid's end.

Be positive, be wise, this virus won't last.
Share memories today of birthday's now past.
A birthday in isolation is no great fun,
But there's worse situations when all is said and done.

You know you can survive it; you know you can cope,
Just keep the faith and live-in hope.
Appreciate all blessings and gifts you receive.
Believe in a bright future, with plenty to achieve.

'Anniversary Antics'

Dedicated to Rod & Deirdre Killeen

50 years of wedded bliss, Ah
Come on now hubby, now give us a kiss.
Years don't matter, it's a wonderful celebration!
Of course, we deserve a standing ovation.

Presents will be opened; cards will be read and
Laughter and tears are bound to be shed.
Memories we share, stories to unfold and
A warning to hubby, "leave some untold."

A creamy chocolate cake is out on display,
50 candles commemorate our day.
Some brilliant blue, others passion pink so
Now give us a moment to a have a think...

A silent wish, let's hope it comes true as
we blow and we puff, again blow and we puff.
Says I to hubby, "I have had enough."
Two candles left; "I'll leave them to you."

Family and friends, they gather about.
Champagne is shaken, popped and poured.
"Happy Anniversary" we hear them roar.

Get the phone, quick, quick, quick!
Photographs are taken, click, click, click.
Everyone comments, we're such a fantastic pair.
As we show off the love, we both still share.

Anniversary antics, there's more and more,
"Ma, Da, step onto the floor." But, the
two of us are reluctant to go.
Such pleading and pleasing, you never saw before.

At last, the two of us, put on a show.
"Go easy love, don't let me go."
As hubby twirls me gracefully, around the room,
he's listening carefully to a familiar tune.

"Remember this one?" he calls me dear
as the music plays and everyone cheers.
"I lubby love, sure how could I forget,
It got to number one, the year that we met."

"What did you wish for," he whispers in my ear.
I look in his eyes and shed a tear.
"I wished for nothing, instead thanked the man above
For sending and leaving me the man that I love."

'I Can't Believe it'

Dedicated to Eithne Dolan Merriman

The thought of being fifty years is shocking news.
It seemed so far away, nowhere near me.
But age was out to find me and
There's nowhere now to flee.
Paranoia has lingered, lingered all the year through.

Now I've reached the date, I can't believe it.
Not a line or crease on my face.
I'm in shock, ah I can't believe it,
I can't laugh now so I'll cry.
The shock makes me quite a nervous wreck,
Seems the more I think about it the more I cry.
But sure, what's the use in crying?
Easier to smile,
Now fiftieth birthdays are in style.

O everyone wants to tell me
That age has served me well,
An entertaining lady through the years.
Yes, this is the date, but I can't believe it.
No, I can't believe it, no…no…

'Father to Daughter'

Dedicated to Margaret Murnane

Now daughter, I say to you,
Life for me is like taking a driving lesson for
It goes to fast,
It goes too slow
And through the traffic lights
And places one should not go at all.
LOST
But all the time
I keep practicing
And reaching crossroads
And turning left and right
And sometimes in the night
Drive where there is no streetlight.
So, daughter don't give up now,
Don't take to the passenger seat
Because you find the lesson tough.
Don't crash now.
You keep driving dear.
You keep practicing.
And you will see
that life is like taking
a driving lesson.

'Glamorous Wife'

Dedicated to Catherine

I am a glamorous wife you know,
No longer 22!
I tend to be chatty, keep smiling broadly too.
Excited and delighted to be part of married life.
That's one of the reasons I'm a loving caring wife!

I wear blue eyeshadow on my eyelids, red paint upon my toes,
Pink blusher on my cheeks, and present a tall elegant pose.
I go to the hairdressers to dye my hair bright red.
That's why I'm a glamorous wife you know, many a person said!

On Fridays, after leaving work, to the city, I go to shop.
Dress after dress I buy, O Lord I cannot stop.
I shop for many hours before deciding to go home,
And know I'm in trouble, when my husband rings my phone.

I love my husband dearly; as he's a very generous man.
Earning lots of money any way he can.
So why change my ways for I can buy what I like
And that's another reason; I'm a very glamorous wife!

‘Another Birthday: I Will Continue...’

Dedicated to Auntie Essie

Will continue to apply nightly,
my Ponds beauty cream.
Rollers, I will twist, into my shiny, straight hair.
Before I sleep and go off to dream.

Soft waves, loose curls I style in my hair
For always, my appearance I will take care.
I’m a glamourous lady, if I may say as
I look in the mirror early each day.

Continue when, the weather allows
To enter my flower gardens full of flowers.
On my knees, pulling weeds,
Cutting, admiring or sowing seeds.

Continue to make toasties of tomato and cheese.
But don’t interrupt me, I beg you please
To race down the hallway to answer the door bell,
Surprised quite often that I never fell.

Five Fine sons, daughters- in-laws dear,
I’m lucky to have them nearby.
Continue to visit whenever they can
For debates, advice from their wise mam.

Continue to enjoy their lingering laughter,
their music and songs thereafter.
Surrounded by a love so real,
young and hearty, I still do feel.

Petite wool coats, I wear so neat and
Ankle boots to warm my feet.
Matching scarves will always wear.
With Beeline lip balm applied with care.

Bus trips to the city, is time just for me.
In Arnott's store, I love to browse for
A dress or coat or brand-new blouse.
I always like to look my best
When meeting in 'Wynns' with special guests.

Continue most of all, to be grateful indeed
For many blessings I have received.
And I thank you too, dear God above
For all the times given with those I love.

'Auntie's Attitude'

Dedicated to Auntie Essie's twenty-five grandchildren

To show off a smile, when times are tough.
keep going, when you've just had enough.
Share with someone how you feel,
Come to realize that time will heal.

To Listen always with an attentive ear.
Can answer with a nod of the head.
Yes, auntie has heard it all before, you see.
Relieved it is not just me.

Be positive, patient and wise.
Pray to God and the saints above,
Before too long you'll receive your prize.
Keep yourself busy each and every day,
She, he or it "is only around the corner," I hear her say.

Auntie's attitude is the right attitude.
Memories, tumble out one after the other.
of a loving wife, devoted mother, caring sister, wise aunt and proud grandmother.
Be thankful for the memories, for happy times outweigh the sad.
To know someone like her, indeed we are glad.

‘Kit Kat Sandwich’

Dedicated to Robin O Connell

A story told to present day,
that it was in the month of May,
The match was over, the home side had won,
so off to the pub to have some fun.
Up at the bar, the brothers lined up;
One, Two, Three Four.
“We’ve won again,” the oldest roared.
Pints of Guinness were ordered first.
Frothy white-pints, to quench their thirst
Continued to drink, wanting more and more.
With singing and music,
they took to the floor.

Then story after story was wittily told.
Contributions made from young and old.
With the help of the Guinness, they laughed aloud.
Well, you never saw such a livelier crowd.
Conversations continued between barman and boys
Until rumbling stomachs caused quite a noise.
A lively character, stood up to announce,
“An auld tasty sandwich is what you need, sure
Come up to my place, and I’ll give you a feed.”
They jumped off their stools with a sudden bounce.
They moved quickly; there was no delay.
‘Follow me up the lane,’ they heard him say.

In his sparse sitting room, he sat the lot.
Then off to make sandwiches and tea piping hot.
Searching cupboards and fridge, no food could he see.
For the wife was on holidays, do you understand me?
The cat, the cat, came to his mind so
Out to the garage where he knew he would find,
Kit Kat food, grabbed off a wooden shelf.
Some Brown chef sauce and some old-fashioned delf.
The food and the sauce, he mixed in a bowl.
Then carefully spread onto blue moulded rolls.
Strange looking sandwiches, he placed on the table.
And told the lads, "Eat all that you're able."

Well to tell you the truth; they ate nine or ten.
You never saw such hungrier men.
Fed and watered, they soon sobered up
after drinking tea, cup after cup.
Thanking him graciously, they took their leave,
And grateful for all the hospitality received.

As sure as I'm standing in front of you mate,
They thought it was tuna sandwiches they ate.
They were so hungry do you understand?
They'd eat anything that came their way.
You can make a sandwich out of anything!
Well, that's what they say.

‘Rendezvous with Whom?

Photo examined one last time,
Content, all will be fine.
Visits to the loo, there have been quite a few.
Lipstick applied and mascara too.

Waiting and watching is now all over.
I sit cross legged and very sober.
He spots me in my summer dress.
Bouncing towards me, asks, “Mary is it…”?

A Tee shirt stretches over his bursting chest.
His belly hangs over jeans of blue.
What I’m in for, I haven’t a clue.
With a sweaty palm he shakes my hand.

An urge to sniff, an awful stench,
What it is? I cannot tell.
Is it bitter bad breath? Is it offensive food?
Sure, what can I say, I can’t be rude.

Just sit over there in front of me!
But from the giant, I cannot flee.
Locked in by the mahogany table.
I’d jump over it, if I were able.

All about him, he blathers and jabbers.
For god's sake, what is he talking about?
O I wish I could go as stiff sighs I push out
Why I'm here? I just don't know!

The smell is getting stronger; I want to sob.
So, I question him, "just what is your job"?
"I'm a mortician"!
Then, continues his tales of those who have died.
While I shout to GOD, "I won't be his bride."

Hand in my pocket: a welcome vibration.
"My phone has saved me," I whisper with elation.
There'll be no rendezvous at any cost!
And I'll pray in purgatory he will...Get Lost.

'Lady's Retirement Pledge'

Dedicated to Phyllis

Retired lady that I am,
My retirement pledge well written.
Sprung to my brain, one night in bed.
It's eloquent, expressive, and easily read.

Pledge never again to get up at seven.
Instead dream away like an angel in heaven.
Laziness, freedom, will do what I please,
Snore loudly. Throw an explosive sneeze.

A morning cocktail to keep me young,
Melting Manuka that clings to my tongue.
Apple cider vinegar, with a vicious taste
And skinny cappuccinos, that narrows my waist.

No bossing, bullology you better believe,
Anyone not welcome can take their leave.
No more ducking, diving, swearing or sweat.
No annoyances, interferences, you can certainly bet.

High heeled shoes will continue to wear.
My love for fashion, will always be there.
Shades of lipstick, on my lips I lay,
Ever ready to face each day

Lavender scented baths, my nightly treat
And beaded bubbles to tickle my feet.
Music to sedate, I go to dream,
After fruity fine wine, or coffee with cream.

Plan each week to try something new,
But where to start I haven't a clue.
A new chapter, a fresh beginning,
All I know is my heart is singing.

A pledge that allows the right attitude,
Informs me infinitely, of how wonderful I
am.
Brave and bold to decide Yes or No.
Pledge honoured when "safely Home to God" I go.

'Waiting...Now Over'

Dedicated to Maria and Jude Quigley

Waiting...waiting...for your dream date to arrive.
Hoping your soul mate soon stands by your side.
Trusting there's a plan, with the Man above,
Appearing out of nowhere, the person you will love.

Will it be this week, this month, this year?
Enjoy the present! Tomorrow is very near.
No wasting time wondering what is to come.
Believe your partner is chosen. God's work is done.

Tomorrow is now the present, in the blink of an eye.
To singlehood; a grand good bye.
To True love forever: a welcome hello.
So much happiness, you both clearly show.

The dream is now a reality for the two of you to share.
Meant for each other! A proud and precious pair!
As you step down the aisle, your faces aglow,
Blessed with a love, that continues to grow!

‘The Choice to Laugh’

A tribute to Olivia Smith R.I.P
Dedicated to her children, Livie, Mary, Tommy and Stephen

Your laughter stretches far and wide,
Not just while by your side.
Staying softly in my mind,
It’s laughter of the richest kind.

We can choose to laugh or not to laugh.
You choose to laugh day after day,
Although, concerns and worries come your way.
You know ‘down days’ come to us all now and then.
So, your laughter enters our hearts to build our hope again.

The gift of laughter is given to us all,
A blessing you use wisely and never stalls.
Laugh, you tell us, when things go wrong,
As wrongs become rights before too long.

“Make me laugh” I ask of you
And my fears and tears soon disappear.
A laughter that brings joy to those you hold dear.
You’re a treasure to have in our presence
From you, we can learn a valuable lesson.

'A Piece of Your Time'

A tribute to my late Father-in-Law Noel McCrann R.I.P.

Now hear you all, you five of mine,
For long enough I gave you, my time.
Now in my later years,
How about a piece of your time?

The daily newspaper on your way to work,
Sure, later on I'll take a look. But if you can't, a sure "musha leave it."
A piece of your time to place a bet, for my love of horseracing, I'll never lose.
A Lucky Fifteen, please help me to choose.

The weekly shopping needs to be done so
A piece of your time to take me to Dunnes.
Bread, butter not forgetting the cake, then on to
'Igoes' to collect the steak, then back to Castle Street for a bite to eat.

A piece of your time at last.
Tell me about your week that has passed.
Around the fire, up at the counter, I sit with you,
Saturday evenings, in JJ's and Tony's bar
Sipping Rum and Blackcurrant, and maybe a Baileys too.

A piece of your time at my hospital bed,
Sometimes cranky, sometimes hot,
Will you bring me an Ice-cream?
from the nearest shop?

Now my days are closing in. All I ask now is a touch of your hand.
For someday at Heaven's Gate, you all will stand.
It is there you will hear me say, all five of mine,
Thank you all for a piece of your time.

'Memories of Mary'

Tribute to Mary Kennedy (neighbour) R.I.P.

A baby girl named Mary, born in Creevyquin
Born to Brigid and Patrick, sister to Nellie,
In fact, she was her twin.
With her sister, brothers, Paddy, Ned and John,
They lived altogether, for many years long.
Known to all, near and far as the Kennedys.

Years passed by and off to work she set,
Mary on her bicycle to do her daily job.
At work in town, some neighbours she met,
Eilish, Carmel, Anne, Maura and Kathleen.
Sure, the craic was only ninety in that bright canteen.

Selected savoury sandwiches, piping pots of tea,
No doubt she played her part on that fine team.
All was served swiftly. including apple tart,
"A Lassie me" that was the routine in the local Mart.
Chatting and joking with famished farmers, she was seen.
Fun and laughter too with Owen in between.

Sociable and outgoing that was our Mary,
Weddings, christenings and birthdays she did attend.
Invited by loving neighbours and long, treasured friends.
On days like these, an effort was made to look her best,
For Mary was fashionable and of course, well dressed.

A warm welcome, a broad smile at her open door.
A quick chat, or an invite in to tell you more,
In the cold of winter
or the bright month of May,
Made time to listen
any time of the day.

At her kitchen window, see her wave through.
Or call a happy hello to me and you.
Spot her, in her summer garden tending her favourite flowers.
Gladly, here she'd spend the sunny hours.
Admiring sweet-scented roses, every colour and kind.
Or kneeling on her "green carpet," one of the neatest you could find.

Arriving now in your summer garden up above
and thinking of you with love
Greeted by family and friends you met along life's way.
Hear them cheer and say like us here today,
"Thank you, Mary, for what you've said and done
May god bless you each and every day."

'Your Eyes'

Dedicated to Bea

Your eyes smile gently on all whom you meet.
Your eyes shine brightly through words that you speak.
Your eyes detect worry shown on a face.
Your eyes relax others at a very quick pace.

Your eyes unveil care for each and every one.
Your eyes exhibit gentleness, comfort, and fun.
Your eyes hold dreams of all you wish to do.
Your eyes play the memories of times old and new.

Your eyes express love for family and friends.
Your eyes speak of kindness that never seems to end.
Your eyes create laughter that extends far and wide.

Your eyes attract others to be by your side.
Your eyes always searching to help those in need.
Everyone needs a friend like you, indeed.

'True Friend'

Dedicated to the lady from Corofin

We work well together, we two.
"Like birds of a feather," me and you.
Same ideas, views, and attitudes.
Appreciative and kind, always in good mood.

Sometimes we turn into drama queens
And perform some magic scenes.
You'd thing we get sense now, at our age
And try to keep drama for the stage.

New chapters, new adventures we look forward to
And dream of wonderful things also coming true.
Give no orders, play no games, tell no lies
Instead, our aims reach for the sky.

Our relationship has taught us
To keep a softer tone and don't bother to moan.
We keep quite calm; we say far less and
realise we don't always have to say yes.

We focus on what today will bring,
Forgetting the past and days to come.
We take every opportunity to have some fun.
We've only got this day when all is said and done.

'Believe Me'

Believe me when I say, the troubles of others are not your fault.
If others blame you, consider it with a pinch of salt.
Believe me, they are looking for attention much of the time.
If they seek your help, well that's just fine.
Jealousy too, can be part of their game,
And set out to take your name.

When others think they are always right,
and wish to fight will all their might,
Believe me, it is better not to react at all.
Never a word did he have to say.
"Just give them a look," I hear Dad say.
Please don't be a victim, don't cry or bawl,
Or into the cute culprit's hands, you'll surely fall.

Believe me; it is important to express how you feel.
Warning, keep it short and sweet. Just stand flat on your feet.
Now show them captain's courage, your beautiful brave face, and state you case.
Believe me, when you do the right thing, say the right thing,
You have nothing to hide and all to graciously gain.
Just every now and then, we must endure some pain.

Revenge, no, no, that is not the way to go,
So be good now, I'm telling you so.

Believe me the experience was meant to be.
There's always a lesson to be learned you see.
Stronger, wiser and confident you will become.
Set for the joyful journey you left off from.

'Giving at Christmas'

Dedicated to Cousin Goretti Killeen

Giving at Christmas, a hard choice to make.
Easier to receive, and easier to take.
"But I can't afford it," I hear you say.
Ah, go on now, make someone's day.

Money, gift or time, just pick from the list.
Please just a little, it won't be missed.
Show some empathy, show some care,
Christmas for many can be so unfair.

Giving at Christmas to those in need,
Won't be forgotten, please sow the seed.
Ease their worry, silence their pain.
Time to light your charitable flame.

Feelings of joy will stir round your heart,
Delighted now, you've chosen to part.
Repaid not always in the way you believe.
Amazed instead by what giving achieves.

'Think...Think'

Think…think about what you say.
Leave untruths far at bay.
Please state only the facts.
Speak with courage, strength and tact.

Think…Think about what you do,
For others, are closely watching you.
Say the right thing or nothing at all.
If unsure, find someone to call.

Think…think about what you hear,
It may bring a smile, or frantic fear.
It may be false; it may be true so
Be still, and silent. Listen too.

Be patient, wait, and do not push for
You will be glad you did not rush.
Time will reveal what is real.
Express then openly how you feel.

"Say Nothing"

Dedicated to Anne Greene Tully

Feel like shouting, screaming or doing something worse
Like firing the odd curse?
Hold it in, say nothing.

Feel like returning an evil comment with another?
You won't realise the impact until horrendous harm is done.
Stop, don't do it, say nothing.

Expressing anger is not the way to go for
It is a quality we don't need to show.
Please say nothing.

Want to make threats because you're upset?
Well, think it through,
For is it really what you want to do?
The answer will come, yes - say nothing.

Wait a while as if you don't give a dam.
Time will return you to a state of calm.
Now, breathe slow and deep.
You'll feel so much better.
Write a letter.

Let your feelings flow.
Then put down your pen and read
Then you will hear yourself shout say nothing.
For now, you realise, the importance of the rule "say nothing."

'Listen to Myself'

Dedicated to Rachel Doran Feeley

Listen to myself.
I know what I want.
I have dreams to realize.
It doesn't matter the size.

I believe I can do it.
No rush, I'll take my time.
Help is always there,
When I say a little prayer.

Others might think
I'm wasting my time.
But I'll show them,
I'll get on just fine.

Challenges, I will face.
It is to be expected.
Calmness and patience,
Will see me through.

I'll do it for myself, nobody else.
For what I do and what I say,
Makes me part of who I am.

Memoir Section

'Daily Spins with Dad'

Dedicated to Claire Finneran

My late dad had a deep love and affection for his job: dairy farming. Wearing his flat-peaked cap and black soiled wellingtons, he took great pride in walking his Friesian cows for their twice daily trip. The trip started in Hanley's field, continued over the Creevyquin Road, up the boreen in front of our family bungalow and ended in the milking parlour that he built himself. He had the company of his sheepdog Lassie and his thick, black, plastic walking stick to keep his cows in tow on their journey.

In the milking parlour, with milking cups in place, the milk flowed through the pipes into a large silver milk tanker. By the time the milking was over, the tanker was full to the top showing a rich "creamy head." A full tanker of milk every morning meant a daily journey to the local creamery in Athleague. Before the journey, my father would take a daily supply of milk from the tanker to be used in the family home. A jug of cream was taken too. It would be poured over freshly baked tarts made by my mother.

While Dad was busy making preparations for his trip, I was busy getting ready for primary school. I was just four years old when I began my schooldays. There were no pre-schools in those days. Primary school for four-year-olds started later in the morning then so this gave me the opportunity to go for daily spins to the creamery with dad before attending school.

With the milk tanker attached to the hitch of his red Hillman Hunter, we were ready to set off for the village creamery. It was a trip I looked forward to every day. During the fifteen-minute drive, my father entertained me by whistling or lilting a familiar tune. Sometimes he sang to me. The song I most clearly remember was the classic hit "Mursheen Durkin" by Johnny McEvoy. In no time, we seemed to have reached our destination: Athleague creamery. While the tanker was being emptied, other farmers and the staff employed at the creamery would pop their head into the front window to say their daily hello to me.

I have to admit it was not the visit to the creamery that I looked forward most but the people I would meet on our return trip. We never drove out of the village without making a stop outside two well-known shops in the village at the time, Connaughton's, on the main street and Finneran's shop beside the local church.

In Connaughton's shop, I would pick my favourite sugary Pastilles or chocolate Rollo's from the shelf. I enjoyed being complimented by the mother and daughter Philly who owned the shop, and I was very proud to be told that I looked just like my dad with my sallow skin and jet-black hair set in pigtails. On other days, we visited Finneran's shop and village post office. It was here, I was greeted by Claire the chatty owner, who was always dressed in her long bright blue shop coat which was a tradition of the shopkeeper at the time. On warmer days, I took time to consider if it would be the multi coloured Wibbly Wobbly Wonder, a yellow and green Loop the Loop or a Choc Ice I would choose from her ice-cold fridge, which was paid for by my generous dad.

Sitting in the back seat of our Hillman Hunter, I would lick and bite into the milk chocolate ice cream or suck slowly on the sticky pastilles. On other mornings, I would stand up between the two front seats to look to the right and left of me and then question my dad as he drove along the village.

"Who lives in that house daddy?"

He patiently gave me the names as he slowed down the speed of the car to point them out to me. He knew them all off by heart. I never had to ask him though who lived in the last building that we pulled up at. No. The tall grey limestone building was the convent primary school where he brought me by the hand to Sr. Eithne's classroom. I knew it was time now to say goodbye to dad and say hello to Baby Infants.

'Father's Fashion Rules

Dedicated to Mary Bannon Hourigan

"Take that off, it doesn't suit you!" This was the frequent order given by my fussy father to my mother and us, his five children, if he did not like the colour, style or shape of an outfit we were wearing. He was definitely no way shy about giving us his personal opinion. And his opinion was usually taken on board and respected.

This dairy farmer had a great eye for clothes fashion. He believed that it was important to dress well as our dress sense may leave a lasting impression on others. He made it his business to take time out from his full-time farming schedule to accompany his wife and family of five on shopping trips. These trips took us to nearby towns to buy one or many outfits on approach to First Holy Communions, Confirmations or wedding celebrations.

Athlone was one of these towns. Burgess fashion store for men and women was often visited to purchase clothes for my mother. Our clothes for 'good wear' as my mother called them were purchased in Eithne O' Rourke's, a small compact children's clothes shop in Irishtown. Eithne ensured that every bit of space in her corner shop was used. Rows of clothes rails displayed a variety of frocks, trousers, jumpers and coats of all colours, shades and fabrics. My siblings and I took our time choosing a suitable outfit. We would sift away to our heart's content through rails of velvet, wool, crepe and cotton and eventually pick out clothes that 'caught our eye.'

And between those rows of rails, we would model these clothes with pride as our father took time to admire us.

"Stand over there in the light, 'till I have a good look at you," he would ask us, pointing his finger in a certain direction.

The light was the natural one that poured in through the front shop window. He would eventually pick his favourite outfit and of course the outfit that we wanted to buy too. No item was purchased before he had eyed them up and down with his grey-green eyes. We accepted that these clothes were to be worn only for 'Sunday Best' after the formal occasion was over.

Clothes worn, must suit the occasion he believed. In the milking parlour, he wore a long olive thick waterproof overall that stretched well below his knees. They protected him from splashes and sprays of liquids that came in his direction. Thin, white or yellow gloves protected his hands from cracks and cuts. Black or green rubber wellingtons were worn in winter and replaced by laced boots in summer. His farmer's cap clung to his head throughout the year. He felt he was not fully dressed without his peaked cap.

During the long winter chill, his rosy cheeks turned a deep purple in colour. His cap jutted out underneath the hood of his heavy padded navy coat ensuring his body had an extra layer of warmth. A wool scarf or mask covered his mouth to protect his lungs depending on the season. One of them was already damaged in earlier years due to the constant inhalation of fertilizer and hay dust.

As a child from 1970s and teenager from 1980s, I can remember my father peeling away layers of his clothing to expose a white vest or Tee shirt worn over belted jeans on hot balmy summer days and evenings. The low-chested, sleeveless vest revealed his sallow skin that had darkened from hours spent in the roasting Roxboro fields. He never wore shorts on the farm. His cobalt blue shorts were confined to Salthill beach or Doon shore in Rockingham, Boyle. Here he sat or lay near the shallow water of the lake or on the beach supervising his children while they swam.

Smart, formal clothing replaced his casual dress code when he finished his farming duties to attend to business in the town such as a visit to the livestock mart, the bank or the local creamery or when he went 'rambling' to friends and neighbour's houses in all seasons.

A wash and shave ritual always took place before getting dressed for these occasions. On leaving the bathroom, smelling of Old Spice my mother would call to him,

"Roger, your shirt is hanging in the hot press."

He would dress himself in the freshly ironed shirt, still warm from the heat of the iron. A Peter England shirt was his favourite brand, pinstripes was his favourite style and blue was his favourite colour. He matched the shirt with cream slacks, navy blazer and matching tie or else with a navy or brown Magee suit. Black leather laced shoes sat underneath the armchair beside the kitchen range ever ready to receive an extra 'kiwi' polish and last-minute shine.

Bent over while sitting in his light brown armchair beside the Stanley range, he would shine his already cleaned shoes using an old woollen sock after polishing them with the kiwi polish. He would then place the sock, the polish, the shoe brush back in the

Jacob's USA biscuit tin which was kept in the nearby kitchen corner press. Now dressed neatly in his blazer or suit and shining shoes he was ready for his last task. He would stand in front of the rectangular mirror which hung on the tiled kitchen wall; and part comb his straight jet-black hair before taking his 'good cap' from the hot press. He placed it with care on his head. His 'good cap' as he called it was kept for socialising, not for farming.

We always knew when dad was ready to take leave from the house as he had a habit of saying to our mother or whoever was present in a confident tone,

"Write she said and she never wrote," as he then reached for the keys of his Opel Record or Hillman Hunter that hung beside the back kitchen door.

'The gentleman farmer' my mother called him, was now dressed to impress anyone he met as he headed off to attend to farming business, visit his relations, neighbours or friends.

And, of course, we, his children would never dream of telling our father that what he wore did not suit him. Well, we never had to.

"Now Lads, This Evening Might Come Wet"

Dedicated to my godson Roger Connelly.

"Now lads, this evening might come wet." This was the usual announcement made by my father as he stood up from HIS chair. The chair was located close to the back kitchen door if he needed to make a quick exit. The announcement came as a gentle hint to his 'workmen' as he called them when it was time to get back to work. Workmen came to our farm to carry out various farming jobs from the beginning until the end of the year. They were quite happy to return to their duties having been served up a four-course meal, home cooked by my mother after ensuring her own 'brood' were "fed and watered" first.

The four-course included soup, a bowl of thick brown oxtail soup and was sometimes poured over the dinner too. It was known as Knorr packet oxtail soup. In fact, for years, I thought it was only soup that existed.

Some days brought the strong smell of bacon and cabbage, bubbling away on our cream Stanley range as it waited to be served and devoured by the hungry hardworking men. The smell lingered in our kitchen for many hours afterwards. O how my father loved the juice of the cabbage as it flowed over of his plate. On other days, my mother served the workmen mincemeat, fried on the pan and flavoured with chopped mushrooms that had been handpicked from our fields. Onions were added also to provide extra flavour. This recipe was served with creamy mashed or boiled potatoes in their jacket. Carrots and parsnips which mother mashed together with melted butter and sprinkled with pepper and salt were served up too. The Friday Ritual: Plaice or Salmon fried on the Stanley range and served with homemade white sauce, tinned Heinz beans and freshly cut homemade fried chips. Meat was never on the menu in our house on that day.

O yes, my mother was noted for her tasty cooking and most of all for her brilliant baking skills. She had my father and his 'workmen' spoilt for choice. Homemade trifle or jelly and ice-cream was served up for desert however we called it "sweet" back in our childhood days. Sweet was a daily treat. To finish off the four courses, she wet a pot of tea for them. A cup of Lyons tea was served with fresh out of the oven fruit scones, rock buns or apple tart depending on what my mother decided to bake on a given day. The workmen, sometimes two, four or maybe six, would sit around the rectangular kitchen table with my father after they had lined up at the aluminium kitchen sink to wash their hands with Palmolive soap. This soap was a permanent fixture beside the kitchen sink. This task 'freed' themselves of some of the odour that they brought into the kitchen with them.

Springtime, brought the choking odour of slurry, which was spread over our lands at Creevyquin. One particular neighbour insisted on being informed in advance so that they could leave the village (as my father called it) for the day while the deed was being carried out. However, this natural 'unwelcome visitor' would stay with us for days. Looking back now, it seemed that my father had a set date, week or month to carry out particular activities on the farm. Nothing or no one would change these dates.

Sheering of the sheep always took place on June seventh every year for many years throughout the Seventies and Eighties. It was a long laborious process. It was a job that required great concentration, skill and plenty of patience. Again, my father had the help of others. Larry Kilroy, who was dad's cousin helped out on the day. He was a tall lanky man with strong arms, full of muscles and veins that looked like they were about to burst. These arms were needed to help hold the ewes in place while being shorn. The seventh of June was special for another reason. It was day I was born and, for years, I could not understand why my father picked my birthday to shear his sheep. I remember asking my mother for a reason on one particular June 7th. She replied swiftly, "Sure wasn't he at a cattle fair, the day you were born."

After the sheep shearing was over, silage making was next on the agenda. This task took place twice a year: The last week in June and the second week of August. From early morning, through the summer evenings until the darkness of the night fell upon them, the 'silage men' cut and transported the green luscious grass in large trailers to our silage pit just a few yards away from our kitchen window. I watched with interest over the Laurel hedge. I would inhale the fresh smell of the cut grass through the open window. It is one of my favourite natural perfumes of the summer season. I observed and listened to the sounds of a huge tractor reversing the trailer while another man called out directions as to when and where to unload the cut grass into our silage pit. Yes, we would be warned to keep out of sight as large tractors and massive trailers approached and left our farmyard during all seasons.

Delays in the cutting of the silage were a frequent occurrence due to the breakdown of machinery. This frustrated my father as time was of the essence. "Time is time" was a phrase I heard him repeat frequently in his conversations on many a subject down through the years. He was concerned greatly that "the evening might come wet" and this would cause further delays in completing the job. The 'silage men' cut our meadow on our farms in Creevyquin and Roxboro. On those days, the only time we saw our father was at mealtimes as he insisted on being present at all times while work was being carried out on the farm. He was at the 'heart and soul' of every project. He believed that a 'man watching was a better than a man working.'

As well as sheep shearing and silage making taking place on the farm, there was also the bale making season. Rectangular bales were the norm when I was growing up. It was a welcome invention for my father who had been through the experience of 'saving the hay' as it was called in his youth. Father, with the help of neighbours and family, cut the meadow with scythes and 'saved the hay' with wooden forks and rakes. These cocks of hay, likes miniature hills dotted the landscape for many a summer season on our farm.

My only experience of rectangular bales was running around the bales in the freshly cut fields playing hide and seek. Later on, when stacked in our hay barn, my siblings and I spent hours climbing up on them, running around them or just lying on them.

Once the baling was over, he was on to the next job: the 'saving of the turf.' And for this job he did not hire workmen to do it. No, he expected his five children to help him instead. It was not a job we looked forward to. My father had ways of getting his children to participate in the tiring repetitive work with comments like, "sure the bog is the best place to get a tan." Like my father, I too, had sallow skin and had jet black hair. Just a few blinks of the sun's rays were enough to darken our skin.

Bending over in the boring bog was back breaking. The hours in hot sunshine, turning the sods to give them a chance to dry was no fun. Days later, we would come back again to pile the dry sods into little stacks. And then at a later date, we were back once again firing the sods into a large trailer to be brought home and stacked neatly at the rear of our pebble dashed bungalow. My mother encouraged us to go too by sending a picnic basket with us. In the basket, she wrapped up ham, cheese and chicken sandwiches flavoured with mayonnaise or mustard. She wrapped them in tinfoil to keep them fresh and provided bottles of red lemonade and tea made up in 7 up glass bottles to quench our thirst. Sultana homemade scones already buttered and coved in homemade marmalade were also included to fill our hungry stomachs. Sitting among the heathers at the entrance to the bog was the most exciting part of the day trip for it was a welcome break from the monotonous work. This food gave us that extra energy needed to keep us going for another couple of hours. And we also got the opportunity to lie on the heather bank to snort in the bog air while we took a well-earned rest.

Apart from seasonal work carried out on the farm, there were also the daily and weekly duties to carry out. Dad milked his Friesians on a twice daily basis. As a child in the early seventies, I can remember the silver milk churns being left at end of our boreen every morning to be emptied into creamery lorries. In later years, my father invested in a silver milk tanker when he increased the number of milking cows and so he brought the milk himself to our local creamery. It was well known as Athleague creamery. He drove the 15-minute journey daily with the milk tanker attached to his red Hillman Hunter and, in later years, in the red Opel Record.

His daily chores had just begun. I can still hear the sound of the yard brush as he tapped the bristles of the brush against the cemented yard or barn and the sound of water being splashed against the ground as he washed down the milking parlours, cow sheds and calf sheds with great care. Nothing was rushed. His milking parlour, yards and barns were kept spotless. It showed us all how much love and respect he had for his animals. Other chores were carried out by my father on his own. These included trips to his local mart. If he was not there to buy or sell, he went along to check out the latest prices of cattle, cows and sheep. Father possessed a great passion and pride for his work and for his animals. Every cow had a name. The name given was associated with the breed, colour or the person whom he had brought the cow from. He would talk to them like they were human and would miss them when they were sold at the mart or went to the factory. In spring time, when baby lambs lost their mother, or were born prematurely, he brought them into our family kitchen and placed them in a cardboard box full of fresh straw. This brought great excitement to us, his children, as our father gave us turns to feed them with a baby's bottle. We would cuddle, rub them and christen them during their stay. They slept close to the heat of our Stanley range and only left our kitchen when they were fit to do so.

His hard work, timekeeping and his passion and pride for farming provided him with a vision. It was a vision to expand his farm at every opportunity. His love for building and plastering was a great advantage to him. He used his skills to expand his farm. And with the help of some of his good neighbours, he built on farm sheds; hay sheds and cattle crushes. And his biggest achievement of all was the building of the slurry pit. I can still remember the excitement when my father had completed the pit. It reminded me of an oversized handball alley and, for weeks, my siblings, neighbours and I would play hand ball down in the deep large open space.

The day of disappointment came though when father announced that the slurry would begin to pour into the pit. Our handball days were over.

Walking around my late father's farm today, one can still see and trace with a finger the imprints that my father made in the wet cement revealing the year a particular building was built. The most treasured imprint of all, even though it is quite faint now is the tracing of my father's finger on the lid of the old cement private well that was built adjacent to our family bungalow. It reads, "1967, Evelyn, 1 year."

This sight intrigued my curious young eight-year-old godson who is called after my father Roger. I showed him the moss-covered lid of the well, one sunny September afternoon. His immediate reaction was to run and find a stick; it was a stick from our last surviving Cherry blossom tree. Wearing army green wellingtons, he rapidly removed the moss using his foot that hid the writing and then began to trace out the letters and numerals with the stick. I stood back smiling and took an immediate notion to video 'the adventure' as my godson called it. It was an adventure that we continued for just another hour for I was conscious of the weather forecast that suggested that "this evening might come wet."

'Temper Tantrum'

Dedicated to all my neighbours and everyone who had to cycle or walk the Creevyquin Road to and from Roscommon town in earlier times.

We are all guilty of throwing temper tantrums at some stage in our childhood. However, I have been left with the impression that I, the eldest of five, was the only sibling in our home who suffered from this malady. To this day, my younger sister reminds in the presence of my mother that "I had an awful temper as a child."

And follows the statement with, "Isn't that right mother?"

She waits with pleasure for my mother's reaction: a broad smile stretches across mother's face followed by a chuckle. My sister continues her onslaught.

"Sure, you could see the evidence for years on your bedroom door."

I supposedly, created dents and splinters from the kicks I

gave the white painted door after been sent to my room for misbehaving. I have no recollection of kicking any bedroom door. In fact, I recall being a very shy child. And very sensitive to comments passed about me: good and bad. When the topic of temper tantrums is introduced, I am swiftly hauled back to 1971 when I was a four-year-old pupil attending the local convent school. I relied on neighbours who lived on the same country road as me when it came to emergencies. The following emergency happened on a fresh February afternoon when I received a half day from school. I should have been delighted with such news but for me this was a day I won't forget for all the wrong reasons.

Two neighbours, who were the same age as I, waited outside the big black wrought iron railings of the school with me, waiting for my mother to arrive to give us all a lift home. Mother did not arrive. Where could she be? I thought to myself. I was only in baby infants for heaven's sake. Surely, she could not forget to collect her darling daughter from school. We had was no phone in our house back then, in fact there was no phone in any house along our road to contact her in those times.

Suddenly, my two neighbours who were the same age as me were joined by their two older brothers. They had arrived from the Christian brother's school having received a half day as well. I can't remember to this day why we got the half day but I will never forget how I got home that day.

The two energetic older boys looked like grown men to us. They had come to escort their baby brothers home. It was obvious that they knew about the half day so there was no excuse for my mother not to turn up to collect us.

"You can walk home with us," they told me.

I had never walked home before. Home was two miles away. And I didn't know these neighbours very well. I was very nervous and shy as I mentioned earlier. I was also very upset and annoyed with my mother for leaving me to fend for myself. I decided I would take the risk and walk home with them. Forty minutes it takes an average adult to walk to our house from that school. For a four-year-old, this was a gruelling unnecessary task.

From the tall black ironed railing of the school and church car park, we set off on our journey through the Sacred Heart church grounds that led us on to Abbey Street. This was the shortcut to the market square in Roscommon town. I tried as best I could to keep up with the longer steps that the boys were taking. The more, I thought about what I was doing, the more nervous I became. A sudden strong urge to go to the bathroom came as we entered the main street. And being painfully shy, the mere thought of announcing to four boys that I needed to get to a toilet fast was mortifying. Veering close to the public toilets in the market square, the urge became stronger. I needed to go the toilet because my bladder could not hold out for much longer.

"Boys can you stop, I need to go to the toilet," I blurted out.

I was expecting them to start roaring laughing, but they didn't. Into the foul-smelling building, I raced to do 'my business'. I came out twice as fast for fear that the boys might have done 'a runner' on me. I was relieved in both ways. Relieved that I found a toilet when needed and relieved that the boys had held on and waited for me. Relaxed, now in their company, instead my thoughts turned towards my mother as I started planning what I was going to say to her when I got home as we continued our journey onto Lanesboro Street, the long Lanesboro Road and finally, Creevyquin, our home address.

No one stopped to give us a lift in their car. And I would probably have refused the offer anyhow. In 1971 there were far less cars on the road. My four-year young legs dressed in white knee socks cotton socks dragged slower and slower. I was finding it more difficult to keep up with the boys. The boys, thankfully, walked past their own homes, delivering me safely up the grassy boreen that led to our bungalow known as "The Laurels."

Although I was exhausted, I was ready to chastise my mother. I tried to turn the handle of the back kitchen door. It was locked.

"Mammy." "Daddy" I shouted. No Answer. I called out louder.

"Mammy…" "Daddy…" The tears began to creep down my face when suddenly I heard a familiar voice. I screamed, "Daddy…" "Daddy…"

It was daddy, laughing.

The back door opened quickly. A guilty look stamped immediately across my father's face.

I began to bawl. And I bawled all evening. A collection of fourth generation photographs of the Killeen family were taken at our home that day. Taking photos of granddad, my uncle, my cousin and his son were far more important than collecting me from school. I was a forgotten child! And excluded from a unique event in our family home. If ever I had a reason to throw a temper tantrum that was surely one of those days.

The Canonization of Blessed Padre Pio-A Roscommon View

This article is a tribute to my father Roger Killeen who was miraculously cured by the now St Padre Pio, to my mother Marie who has devoted much of her spare time to the spreading of devotion to this saint, to many of my friends who asked me to keep them in my prayers, to Reena and Chris both of who travelled with us on the trip, and to one Kathleen who would have dearly loved to be at the canonization but had to cancel due to ill health.

My mother, sister Sandra and I travelled to Rome on June 13th 2002 with Joe Walsh tours to take part in a five-day pilgrimage of Rome, the climax being the canonization of blessed Padre Pio on Sunday June 16th. From the time we arrived in Rome until the time we left on Monday June 17th, we were blessed with beautiful weather, often too hot at times.

During our pilgrimage, we stayed at the hotel Palladium under the care of helpful and friendly staff. Over the days, we became friendly with the other forty-six members of our group. Many of them shared stories with us relating to how Padre Pio had touched their lives.

Among the friends we met, was a local resident called Patricia who brought us to see many buildings, sculptures, fountains and brought us to events that were not on the official itinerary. She escorted us to the oldest basilica in Rome known as the 'Basilica di Santa Prassede' which contains the column of the flagellation of Jesus Christ. Many flock here to have their relics blessed. From here, we travelled to see the beautiful basilica known as the Basilica Santa Maria Maggiore' to attend a mass to celebrate St. Anthony's feast day. This Basilica houses the manger that St. Joseph built for Jesus and is located in front of the main altar.

On our second day, we were up bright and early to visit the Vatican City to receive a guided tour of the most famous city in the world known as St. Peter's Basilica. There is much to see in the Basilica including the chapel of the Pieta which is named after Michelangelo's famous marble structure. This chapel is protected by a bullet proof glass due to incident in the early 1970s's when a 'crazy man' entered the chapel and destroyed the head of Our Lady with a hammer.

On the fifteenth, the majority of the group went to visit Assisi but our family and close friends opted to stay in Rome to see more of the local wonderful sights.

We went to see the 'Scala Santa' which contains the flight of stairs which was ascended by Christ when he was judged by Pilate. We climbed the 28 steps on our knees, stopping on each one to say a prayer. Some of the steps are imbedded with relics containing the blood of Jesus Christ.

Our next trip was to take part in a Latin mass celebrated by a very holy priest which proved to be a very moving experience for us all. Later, we paid a visit to a tiny church called 'Chiesa del

Domine Quo Vadis'. Here, we saw the footprints of Jesus Christ on the ancient Via Appia. From there, we went to the Grotto of the Three Fountains located in Via Laurentina in Rome. It is here Our Lady appeared in 1947 to a Bruno Cornacchiola and his three children. She became known to them as "Our Lady of Revelation." She appeared to them holding a book close to her heart which contained the story of Revelation-the Bible.

Towards the rear of the grotto, there is a tunnel containing plaques and prayers of thanksgiving from people of all ages addressed to Our Lady for the numerous miracles they have performed for them. Photos of such pilgrims cover the walls of this tunnel and candles can be seen alight both inside and out. Bruno, now 89 returns to the grotto once every month to retell his story of the apparition as if it only happened yesterday.

Even though we were very tired from the scorching sun, the continual walking and the travelling by car, we were adamant that we would not return to the hotel without paying a visit to downtown Rome to see the famous 'Spanish Steps.' It is a popular place for newlyweds to have their photograph taken. We finished our tour of the city by visiting the Trevi Fountain. Here, one gets the chance to make three wishes by sitting with one's back to the fountain and throwing a coin over the shoulder. The most popular wish is that one can return to Rome.

After a hectic day, we retired to bed early to prepares ourselves for a very early rise as we were about to attend the most important event of the pilgrimage: -The canonization of Blessed Padre Pio.

We arrived Sunday morning at the Vatican at 7.15 am. We were unfortunately too late to get a seat at the Piazza. (St Peter's Square) It was already jammed with devotes of Blessed Padre Pio. In soaring temperatures, thousands of us waited patiently, protecting ourselves from the sun with multi coloured hats and umbrellas.

The ceremony commenced at 10am. At 10:30am, there were loud cheers, clapping and waving of flags when John Paul 11 declared in Latin that Blessed Padre Pio was now "inscribed in the annals of the saints." And in the entire church he would be honoured with devotion among the saints. St Padre Pio who bore the stigmata, the wounds of our lord, who was endowed with supernatural gifts like bi-location (the ability to be in two places at once), who could predict the future and heal the sick would have his feast day celebrated on September 23rd.

The extreme temperatures of 35 degrees Celsius proved too much for many of the pilgrims as they suffered sun stroke. As a result, they had to leave the ceremony before it concluded at 12: 30pm.

That evening, a free classical concert took place in the auditorium followed by fireworks display in St. Peter's Square. Unfortunately, many of the group including myself were too tired to make a return journey to witness the special celebrations.

The following morning, the last day of our trip, we said our goodbyes to the staff at the hotel and set off once again to the Vatican to attend a thanksgiving mass in the auditorium which is adjacent to St. Peter's Basilica. The mass was celebrated in Latin. A big surprise awaited us when the mass was over as Pope John Paul 11 arrived unexpectedly onto the altar. At once, everyone in the auditorium stood up on their sears, clapped their hands and shouted out continually "Papa…" "Papa…"

Others took photos and videoed the event. The pope spoke to the congregation for half an hour however he did not speak in English. I was not disappointed. The atmosphere was good enough for me. Following his speech, a number of invalids were assisted onto the altar to meet him.

While the pope blessed, and spoke with these special people, the audience broke into song, singing the well-known hymn "Ave Maria." I have to admit that this was the most emotional and overwhelming event of the five days. As I looked around me, there were people wiping away tears from their eyes indicating how much Pope John Paul 11 was loved and cherished by everyone present.

Reluctant to leave the wonderful scene, we had to quickly rush back to our bus because we were invited to tea and biscuits in the Irish College and to meet many of the Irish priests who were based in Rome. This was our last stop before heading to the airport for our flight home.

For my family and I, those five days had been a wonderful experience. A visit to Rome is one that I would advise everyone to avail of at some stage during their lifetime. It was my first trip to Rome and I hope it won't be my last.

This Memoir was published in Roscommon Champion (5th July 2002)

Roscommon Classes of 1984 Enjoy Joint School Reunion

This memoir is dedicated to the all the past students of the Vocational school now (Roscommon Community college), Christian Brother's School and the Convent of Mercy Roscommon who were unable to attend the 1984 joint class school reunion and Johnny Horan, Fiona Feeley and Ciara Naughton staff members at Horan's restaurant who cared for us into the early hours of the morning.

The long-awaited reunion night of the class of 1984 that we so looked forward to had finally arrived. The four months of preparation had been completed. The phone calls had been made, the cheques and cash had been collected and the tickets for the event had been posted. Luke and Fiona Mannion of Sunshine Videos, DJ Noel Finnegan and Gerard O Loughlin photographer had all been booked for the historic occasion.

On December 27th 2004, past students headed out on a windy night towards Johnny Horan's brightly lit function room on the Racecourse Road. The excitement was building higher and higher in the function room as the members of the reunion committee sat and waited eagerly to meet their old classmates and old admirers of 1984. Thoughts began to rush through our mind. 'Would we recognise our old school friends? Would they recognise us?'

For some of us, this was going to be our first meeting with many of the past students since we left school all those years ago.

We were soon to find out as they began to stroll through the reception doors promptly at 9pm. Some approached with blank expressions on their faces. There was no recognition what so ever. However, on revealing the name 'Evelyn,' the blank faces were replaced by smiles. Introductions were exchanged, hands firmly shaken and backs were clapped.

These moments were captured on camera by Gerard O Loughlin photographer as the past students from each school smiled broadly for the camera. One could not help notice how glamourous all the ladies looked. They had made the same effort as they had done so for their graduation dance twenty years previously.

After the photo call, it was time to serve up the hot and tasty buffet which Johnny Horan and his diligent staff had prepared for us. Once the meal was over it was time to move swiftly on to the reunion speech. I began by welcoming all the past students to the first every joint school reunion in Roscommon town. I thanked all the past students who had travelled from villages, town and cities across Ireland and abroad for the unique event.

I gave special thanks to the past students who helped with all the preparations. Firstly, the Reunion committee. Eithne Dolan Merriman. Rachel Doran Feeley, Howard Simpson, Niall Croghan and Johnny Horan. Donie Harlow was thanked for his help in the identification process of the CBS past students and providing their addresses. Sean Conniffe was thanked for his kindness and generosity. It was he took responsibility for the typing printing and the assembly of the reunion booklet. Michael Earley was thanked for his unlimited knowledge of phone numbers of many of the past students.

After every one was thanked, we had a minute's silence for all the past students who, sadly, had passed away over the years. And, we had a roll call of all the students present.

It was then time for the music and dancing to commence. DJ Noel reeled us back to the summer of 1984 when the boy band "Wham" topped the charts with "Wake Me Up Before You Go Go." The hits were even rolled back to the 1960s as we danced to Brendan Boyers classic "The Hucklebuck."

The atmosphere was electric as everyone joined in, dancing, rocking and jumping to the sounds of the songs from the 1980s.

We took a break from the dancing when a 14-inch fresh cream cake was rolled onto the centre of the dance floor. Twenty blue candles flickered on top. Each one symbolizing a year since leaving school. The music returned with the blasting sound of AC/DC for our rock enthusiasts. This followed with hits from the bands that played in the Race club on the Racecourse Road when were very young teenagers.

Another break was taken so that I could invite all the new mammy and daddies of 1984 up to the DJ box to present them with practical baby presents.

The music played well into the early hours of the following morning as we jived, rocked and sang to our heart's content. The concluding song from the well-known rat pack member Frank Sinatra brought everyone out on to the dancefloor. We all gathered in a circle and swayed and sang to "New York, New York." The six hours passed by far too quickly. By the time the reunion was over, we felt we had all known each other for the past twenty years. Slowly and reluctantly the majority of us bid our farewell to the classmates of 1984; Those whom we met on a regular basis and to the newly acquainted past students that we were delighted to have met.

The rest of us stayed on chatting for another few hours before walking back together along the Racecourse Road to the town centre. On the trip, we could not help but think about our school graduation of 1984 for it had all the features of the night. Just like our graduation ball, this night had been a roaring success. By the time we had reached the market square, we were feeling rather hungry so we made a 'beeline' for Regan's bar and restaurant which opened early in the morning. Having immediately spotted a blazing fire on entering, we all huddled around it while we made our order for a full Irish breakfast. By the time the breakfast arrived we were too tired to speak instead we sat silently while we tucked into our large fry.

As soon as our breakfast was devoured, it was time to order our taxis home. We said our goodbyes. We would never forget our joint school reunion of December 27th 2004.

Article published in Roscommon Herald January 26th 2005

'Second Miracle'

In memory of Marian Hanly and Agnes Donnellan

Dedicated to all devotees of St Padre Pio, to those who have received blessings and miracles through his intercession and to those devotees who are praying to him with faith that he will answer their prayer. I am dedicating 'Second Miracle' especially to the following:, Eileen Mannion, Geraldine Sheridan, Ena Lynch, Josie Banahan.

The New Year of 2003, did not start off well. A friendship of 20 years had been snatched away for me on the last Saturday in January. Lethal ice, hard snow and freezing temperatures that covered the landscape added to my heartache. The following Monday, I attended the funeral of my friend Cathy. I stood silently, observing the petite curly headed lady with 'doll like features sleeping in the coffin.' She had lost so much weight due to the dreaded disease…Cancer. A large lump tightened my throat as I identified St. Padre Pio's red rosary beads wrapped loosely around her intertwined little fingers. I had presented them to Cathy after returning from the canonisation of the saint the previous June, just a few weeks after she had been diagnosed.

A further diagnosis had also been delivered in my local hospital to my father Roger earlier that January, who was a patient now since New Year's Day. It was pneumonia once again. My father's lungs had been suffering for many decades. The spreading of lime on the land and the shaking of hay dust on the floor of the stables and barns on his farm for years with no protection had a consequence. He now had only one healthy lung. The other, just existed.

It was now the fourth week of my father's stay in a six bedded medical ward. This stay was much longer than usual. Each evening after work, I made the routine visit to the hospital with my mother. At this stage, there was not a ward or a bed in the hospital that my father had not lay in due to his repetitious encounter over the years for his medical needs.

Over the years, the usual procedure followed. A trip to the hospital by ambulance and greeted frequently by my sister who worked in casualty. A diagnosis of pneumonia was identified. His arms were poked and prodded many times before being attached to an intravenous drip as doctors tried to get to get a cannula into a suitable vein. His arms always displayed a colour of deep purple and mustard yellow from the procedure. A concoction of medication was added to those he was already taking and then ushered at some stage to a medical or surgical ward depending on availability of beds.

Two of my sisters were nursing in the hospital that particular January, so he was surrounded by the extra love, attention and care that he needed...so, we all believed.

On the last Saturday afternoon of that January, I realised that I needed time out for myself.

'Some retail therapy may ease my stress,' I thought. I made the decision to go on a shopping spree to Athlone.

I had just parked my little Ford Fiesta in the shopping centre car park, when my Nokia phone jingled in my handbag. My hand began to shake as I fumbled for the phone. My immediate guess was that it was someone from the hospital calling. I was correct. I recognised the familiar phone number before answering. I sensed that it was news that I did not want to hear.

In a rushed voice, my youngest sister who was on duty burst out.

"Evelyn, where are you? Please, please come to the hospital quickly. Father is refusing to take his medication and he will not eat his meals. He always listens to you," she added.

I paused before replying

"I'll be there as quick as I can," I said and hung up.

My family believed that I was the only sibling who could calm him down. I, the eldest of the family, felt that that it was my duty to be close to my father when he needed me.

No chance for retail therapy. No chance for solitude. Instead, I was the one to get the opportunity to cheer up my upset father and try to put him at ease. An immediate saying of my father popped into my head.

"Time is Time."

It was time to leave Athlone straight away to be by my father's side. As I drove back, the question rolled over and over in my mind. 'Why was he not eating or taking his medication?'

I rushed into a six bedded hospital ward that evening to find my father lying motionless under the bedclothes. He was no longer agitated however his complexion was pale. On calling his name, his eyes opened and a faint smile crossed his pale face. I sat down on a green leather armchair adjacent to his bedside. Moving my head close to his, I kissed him on the forehead before asking him softly,

"Why won't you eat your meals and take your tablets, Dad?"

Holding his right hand, still warm from being huddled underneath the bedclothes, he whispered slowly.

"He has told me to fast."

"Who has told you to fast?" I asked with curiosity.

"St. Padre Pio," he replied.

A shiver ran through me. I had read St. Padre Pio biography and was aware of the importance he placed on fasting to aid healing. It all made sense.

St. Padre Pio had played a major part in my father's life since August 1979. At the age fifty-four, my father was diagnosed with leukaemia in a Galway hospital. He was instantly cured of the disease during his stay. A lady visiting dad's ward remarked that a fabulous fragrance of roses had engulfed her on entry to his private room.

"There are no roses here," my father informed her.

The smell known as the odour of sanctity suggests that some form of healing is taking place. Although not a saint in 1979, he had performed many miracles both during his life time and since his death in 1968.

A few weeks after his miraculous recovery, St. Padre Pio appeared in a vision to my father at the foot of his bed at home. The saint spoke to him. He gave him a tough task. He asked him to share the story of his miraculous recovery in public. My father answered him.

"I will do anything for you, but I beg you, please do not ask me to stand up in public to tell my story."

Dad surprised himself as he eventually found the courage to carry out the task. He did stand up and give a witness talk at a Cursillo prayer group in Donamon Castle, Roscommon with the support of his friends who included Ena Lynch. He informed those present of the miraculous cure from leukaemia he received through the intercession of St. Padre Pio.

Twenty-four years later, St. Padre Pio was back to give my father another personal message. Well, an order I believe. Dad, too, had a way of giving orders in a diplomatic way. And he was also capable of taking them too. I truly believed that the last Saturday in January was the beginning of a process that would lead to a second miracle for dad. I sat at my father's bedside from the early hours of that Saturday evening until the early hours of Sunday morning, listening to his shallow breathing and praying to the saint for his recovery. My concentration was interrupted now and again by patients snoring loudly or coughing harshly in the six bedded ward across from the nurse's station. He slept from 9pm that night and was still sleeping at 8am the following morning when I slipped away from his bedside to return home. My dear friend Cathy died that Saturday. It was not until the following day that I received the shocking and upsetting news from a friend. I could not bring myself to visit dad that Sunday.

Monday evening, I accompanied mother and my youngest sister to visit dad earlier than usual as I was heading off to attend Cathy's funeral.

"My fast had come to an end!" he announced to us. And immediately, ordered his wife and daughter to go the local chip shop to buy him chicken and chips. My mother and sister looked at one another and smiled. They agreed to go and purchase the food while I agreed to stay on to keep him company. Dad was sitting in the forest green leather armchair to the right of his hospital bed while I stood in front of him chatting. Our conversation stopped abruptly with an order from dad.

"Don't look now Padre Pio is standing behind you."

When dad gave an order, one always obeyed and that Monday was no exception. I didn't look. I was afraid to look. I believed the saint was standing behind me. This was a moment I would not forget. Such a unique experience had never happened to me before and I thought such an experience may never happen to me again.

'If I look around, he may disappear,' I thought to myself. I did not want to upset my father or St. Padre Pio either. He gave no message this time. '*Was this more evidence that St. Padre Pio was going to perform a second miracle?'* I thought excitedly.

The next day, I got an urge to ring Marian Carroll. This special lady was seriously ill when she was miraculously cured by Our Lady of Knock Shrine in September 1989.

'Surely her prayers would be heard quicker than mine' I convinced myself. A visit from her would cheer him up too.

The date of the visit was decided: Friday, February 7th 2003. Marion came to the hospital to pray with dad. I was at work. When I arrived home that evening, my mother reported to me that Marion Carroll did not have any hope for father's recovery. Friday's news was devastating. Dad's sickness just seemed to drag on and on.

Sunday felt different. It was bright day with a fresh breeze. The blinding sun caused me to pull down the sun visor as I drove to the hospital. And I had a feeling of positivity as I entered the dad's ward. Another patient lay in my father's bed. A nurse on duty approached me.

"Your father has been moved to a private ward, he's in room number two," she informed me.

She gave no reason why and I didn't ask for one. Opening the door of the private room slowly, the loudness of the television grabbed my attention. Then my mouth opened wide when I saw my father sitting up in bed with two white plump pillows tucked behind his back. His hands were clasped loosely over the fresh white bed sheets. His grey green eyes were now bright and alert. His cheeks had returned to a rosy pink colour. I looked towards the television. Horseracing was being televised live from Leopardstown Racecourse. Yes, I remembered straight away, it was Hennessy Gold Cup Day and there was the horse called *"Beef or Salmon"* the favourite, trotting around the parade ring. Dad always had a deep love for horses. Breeding mares and foals for show jumping was a hobby he loved. He dedicated some Saturday afternoons to watching horse racing on television over the years when he wasn't busy on the farm.

"Hello, dad," I called out excitedly. No reply. Dad was zoomed into the commentary of the horse racing.

"Dad…" "hello…" I called again.

He looked up at me, smiled and beckoned on me to come in.

I made myself comfortable on the green leather armchair located beside his bed to watch the race with him.

'This is a great sign,' I whispered to myself.

The race began.

After a few seconds into the race, I asked him with great enthusiasm,

"What price is '*Beef or Salmon*' dad," regretting that I hadn't placed a bet.

"Shush" came his swift reply.

I put my hand over my mouth to stop a roll of laughter escaping as I sat and continued to observe my father full of pride, shouting and roaring "come on *Beef or Salmon.*" I knew there and then that my prayers had been answered. St. Padre Pio had definitely worked a miracle over the weekend. The new year may not have started off well however it all ended exceptionally well in February for my family and I.

"*Beef or Salmon"* won the "Hennessy Cognac Gold Cup." And most importantly, dad was a winner too.

He had "beaten" pneumonia at last and was back to his good old self. St. Padre Pio had performed a second miracle for my dad and I'm convinced my spiritual friend Cathy and Marion Carroll's prayers helped with his recovery too. My father was discharged from hospital three days later on February 12th 2003 after six long weeks. I had now a valuable friend in heaven to pray to and my family and I were privileged to gain three and half more special years with our father.

'While Sitting in Dad's Chair...'

Dedicated to Mary Greene

I brought it back to my family home having received an almost complete make over. It has been part of the family kitchen for many years. I cannot remember exactly when it arrived into the kitchen, however, I do remember that it replaced a homemade rectangle turf box. I stood there admiring the colour of the fabric I had chosen for it: Russet brown. It was the closest I could get to the original colour. I love its soft, smooth and velvet like texture. The wooden arms and legs were still slightly scratched and dull due to years of usage but that did not bother me. Pledge repairing oil would quickly restore the arms and legs to its original gloss. I placed the chair back snugly between the chocolate brown and biscuit coloured Stanley range and the white aluminium back kitchen door. And then I sat into it. Dad's chair.

I call it dad's chair because he was the only one who sat in it. By pure co-incidence, the chair had come back to stay on the eve of my late father's birthday. And there was another co-incidence, the chair had been upholstered by the son of his dear friend Denis. I sat peacefully on its firm cushion that autumnal October evening observing the sun flashing through the kitchen window. And as I sat there, images of dad began to flash like the sun into my mind.

I could see him sitting in the chair polishing his laced shoes. A page from an Irish Independent newspaper lies on the terracotta tiled kitchen floor. Upon it, lies a tin of kiwi polish, a polish brush, a J cloth and an old sock. He used the J cloth to clean his black or brown laced shoes while the old sock gave his shoes an extra shine. I began to smile to myself as I recalled a photo, I took of him one Sunday morning while he was polished his shoes for mass. I always remember what he said to me.

"Have you nothing else to be doing? go and get ready for mass," he ordered. He never went to mass without polishing his shoes. And he was never late for mass.

I could picture him on Saturday nights, sitting cosy, legs crossed in the chair listening to a traditional Irish music programme on RTE Radio 1.

He did not like to be disturbed while he tapped his feet and whistled to jigs, reels and hornpipes. Sharon Shannon's tune "Blackbird" made him jump out of the seat to turn the radio up higher. Now and again, he'd break into a form of traditional singing called lilting.

"Dom de diddle dom, dom de diddle…"

I had no interest in these repetitive rhythmical, traditional songs, however, I was amused by the contentment and relaxation this one-hour programme brought to him.

On wintery evenings, while seated in his chair enjoying the blast of heat coming from the Stanley range, I could see him observing mother frying rashers, sausages and eggs for the family tea on the range. Sometimes she treated us to liver and fried potato, left over from dinner time. On many occasions, spits of margarine from the frying pan fired in his direction due to the closeness of his chair to the range. Dad would put his hand up to protect his face and tell mother to move the pan further over to avoid being burnt by the grease.

"Can't you sit at the kitchen table Roger; the tea will be ready soon," she often suggested, but he never moved. A large silver kettle was also a permanent fixture on the range. I began to laugh to myself when I recalled the reaction of dad when steam from the spout of the kettle aimed for his face. Leaping from his chair, he would mutter curses to himself as he quickly turned the kettle in the opposite direction to save himself from a steam burn.

I recalled sad images too of dad that evening. The last couple of years of his life were spent sitting for many hours in HIS chair. After days, sometimes weeks in hospital recovering from pneumonia or a chest infection, he returned home to be close to his family and close to the heat of the Stanley range. No longer able to participate in his farming activities, he instead observed mother baking his favourite recipes on a daily basis. He looked forward to tasting her homemade brown bread for breakfast, piping hot vegetable soup at dinner time and her hot fruit scones or apple tart served with a cup of tea after dinner.

These flashing images have convinced me that dad had found great comfort while sitting in his russet brown chair. Now, it's my turn to find comfort while sitting in dads' chair.

'The Wonder of Mother'

Dedicated to my goddaughter Ellie Jane Carthy

"*And you're always there to lend a hand in everything you do,*
That's the wonder, the wonder of you" …

Sang my mother softly as a contestant performed Elvis Presley's classic during Ireland's Got Talent TV show. I was immediately inspired to video this event. The 1970s lyrics make me reflect over the number of times my mother lent her hand to others.

Mother was born in the town of Moate, Co Westmeath, the daughter of a garage owner. I wonder how a young single girl was willing to lend a hand to manly duties such as changing tyres and oil in her father's business. I wonder how she showed such a love for Lawn Tennis and became a competent player when her children showed no interest in participating in the sport. It was at the Carmelite Tennis Club in the town where she defeated many an opponent. Her expertise led her to win a perpetual trophy at the age of twenty-one.

Not only did she play tennis to keep fit, she danced five nights a week to showbands who travelled to local carnivals. The local Roseland ballroom in Moate and the Fairyland ballroom in Roscommon were just two of many places that she danced in.

I wonder how mother initially coped when she transplanted herself from town world and tennis lawns of Moate to a village farm house when she married dad in 1965. She swapped her tennis and dancing shoes for knee high wellingtons and took on the challenge of farming life.

I wonder how she survived as a young mother in her early thirties in a country village where many of her neighbours were single, elderly men and woman. She also took great care of her elderly mother and father-in-law who lived with us while rearing her children, during the 1960s and 1970s.

Her elderly neighbours only form of transport was their bicycle. It was a time when not many women in the area developed the skill of driving. Mother's driving skill allowed her to help her neighbours when needed.

Mother developed many skills over the years. I believe her best skill was baking. My siblings and I could not wait to get home from school to burst into the kitchen to see what freshly baked items mother had displayed on the wire tray. The dozen golden high peaked queen cakes never got a chance to cool. The warm spongy Madeira mixture was quickly devoured by us starving students. We would rearrange the buns on the tray, believing that she would not notice five had disappeared. Homemade brown bread, wrapped in a hand towel to keep the crust soft was observed turned it upside down on the tray daily. We could not wait to cut through the cross she placed in the raw bread earlier with a bread knife. Thick slices of warm bread, buttered and smothered with homemade marmalade kept our hunger at bay while we waited for dinner. Of course, she often caught us in the act.

"How many times do I have to tell not to touch the bread before your dinner?" she would ask us.

One day, to surprise mother, I decided to make queen cakes. I began whipping the butter and sugar together in her toffee-coloured crockery bowl. Holding the grooved bowl on its side with my left hand on the Formica kitchen worktop, I began to beat the mixture with the wooden spoon. I whirled the mixture around and around, faster and faster. Suddenly, the bowl toppled off the kitchen work top onto the floor. Chips of the bowl and the mixture splashed everywhere. I fumbled in the kitchen drawer and found a spatula to scrap the creamily vanilla looking mixture off the floor. Engrossed in the messy task, I failed to see mother enter the kitchen.

"Do you know what, you'd break iron," stated the familiar voice.

Mother immediately rushed to help me remove the pieces of her broken crockery bowl from the terracotta tiled floor. While doing so, she added another one of her repetitious phrases,

"You newdy nawdy!"

I never knew what the phrase meant until I recently googled it.

It actually means "weak."

I wonder now why she used this phrase at all.

I never wondered after that incident why she made all her baking mixtures in a plastic bowl.

Mum no longer uses her plastic baking bowl, drives or works on the farm. She lives in a nursing home. It is now the turn of her daughters to lend their hands. We drive her to our homes, the family home of over fifty years and to her hometown. We bake her apple tarts, sultana scones and queen cakes and serve them to her during her visits.

When we ask her

"Would you like apple tart, a scone or queen cake, Mum,"

She replies politely,

"I don't mind."

We, her daughters smile, because we do not wonder why she has never lost the taste of delicious home baking.

'What is in The Cadbury's Dairy Milk Box?'

Dedicated to auntie Nollaig Grogan Kelly

I have always known since I was a teenager that it was hidden away on the top shelf of the hot press in what was then our 'old kitchen.' Over the years, I was tempted to take a peek into that box while searching for bedlinen or eiderdowns. These were kept on the lower shelf. I was afraid to take it down to indulge in its contents for if I was caught, my mother's frequent order would be heard very quickly "put that back where it belongs" so I never got the opportunity to find out what was in the Cadbury's Dairy Chocolate box until a few months ago.

What an assortment did I find in that box one blazing summer's May evening when the Cadbury's chocolate box bounced back into my mind. I was sitting peacefully in the television room. I had the whole house to myself as it now unoccupied. The timing was perfect. I had all night to chew on the contents of violet rectangular box. The only sound coming through the window was the braying of the mare and foal coming from the back field.

A different sound soon entered my head on opening it because the first item that grabbed my attention was the lyrics of Brendan Boyer's big hit "I Ran all the Way Home." Mum had handwritten the lyrics on a sheet of notepaper. I could immediately hear my mother singing the song in my mind. The next item that stared out at me was a two-inch square piece of paper with a signature on it. I began to read it. I could not believe the co-incidence. It was an autograph from Brendan Bowyer who had died that same week. It read "To Marie with love Brendan Bower.' It brought a soft tear to my eye as my mother would not be able to read this autograph now due to her poor eyesight.

What else was there to be found in this box now fifty-five years old? Since mum married dad in 1965, the sweet box has slept quietly until I awoke it with a bang. What aroused me most of all was the wedding present list that my mother had also handwritten on a sheet of note paper. She had taken down the names of all the gifts that she had received from her family and friends.

"What?" I called out to myself as I read the list slowly. A corner China cabinet, a gift to mum and dad from her mother. This cabinet was not bought but instead passed on from one generation to the next. A hostess two-tiered trolley was the gift from her oldest sister Carmel, while the two fire log boxes were a gift from her brother Mossie. Also included in the list were China full sets and half sets, bedsheets, napkins, drinking glasses and cutlery from various other members of the family and friends of my parents. Only one present of money was received in dollars. It was a present from her younger brother Oliver who had emigrated to the States. I wondered who would accept such simple presents nowadays. Wedding couples today expect money as a wedding gift. Well, many of those simple wedding presents are still treasured in our family home. That corner mahogany cabinet with its gold satin lining still stands well-polished and still holds those China half sets and glasses received on my parent's wedding day.

The Cadbury's dairy milk box holds their wedding telegrams too. Dark mustard in colour, they read "To Marie and Roger," best wishes, from guests that could not attend the wedding. The notes are brief. Each word cost money. Some are typed, others are handwritten and show the address of the hotel, "The Shamrock Lodge hotel," Athlone.

This hotel was a popular venue for dinner dances which mum and dad attended when they were single and married. One of her engagement cards in the box reveals a surprising piece of information. Her friend Ena comments that she was disappointed that mum did not mention their engagement at a dinner dance that they attended there, the previous week. However, she suspected there was something up by the behaviour of my mother and father.

Mum's secret box contained plenty of surprises and no shocks thank God. The sweetest surprise of all were the blue and pink religious badges of "Our Lady" and the "Sacred Heart". These were attached to our baby carry cot with safety pins to keep us, their five children safe while we slept.

What was I going to do with all these treasures? I did not have to think for long. I was going to photograph them onto my phone and read out pieces to my dear mother during my visits through the window of the nursing home where she resides. Instead of telling me "Put the box back where it belongs," mum melts with happiness because these treasures bring her back to the people of her youth, her memories of the showband era and when she met and married my father. And finding out what was in the Cadbury's Dairy Milk box was definitely worth the wait.

From Family Home to Nursing Home

Dedicated to my siblings Peter, Sharon, Siobhan and Sandra And my mother's grandchildren Charlie, Ellie Jane, Jessica, Abby, Rachel, Roger, Luke and Brendan.

We never thought the day would come when we would have to speak to our dear mother through the window of a nursing home. Before cursed Covid-19 took that privilege away from us, we, her doting daughters took turns to sit her by the hot turf fire in her family home or at our own homes to be "spoilt rotten."

"Are you warm enough, mum?" we would ask her as she sat close to the open fire while we flung on the extra sod of turf or shovelled in more coal to keep her extra cosy. She also enjoyed sitting in her late husband's armchair beside the Stanley range in her own home while her daughter cooked the Sunday dinner.

"What would you like for dinner mum?" we would ask her. Her repetitious reply in her usual placid voice was always the same.

"I don't mind."

Her favourite dishes were Roast Beef, Lasagne, Grilled Salmon or Lemon or lime chicken, with plenty of vegetables of course added to the plate. Peas were never offered. She never liked them. All dishes were served to her with creamy mashed potato gravy or sauce over those wonderful weekends.

We never asked her what she would like for dessert? We knew exactly what she liked. A large of slice of apple pie with custard or cream, homemade fruit scones, fruit cake or some sherry trifle. These deserts were always served to her with a cup of Lyons tea after her dinner. The fact that she was a diabetic was totally ignored at weekends.

When we look back now, we realise how precious those weekends were, spent in the company of our dear mother.

During the summer sunshine, she lay on the sunchair in our back gardens, wearing her dark brown sunglasses, licking an ice-cream cone or sometimes sipping Club Orange or 7 Up. On such occasions, she was happy just listening to the sounds of her grandchildren playing football in the nearby field. She got much enjoyment too from observing and listening to the sounds of her grandchildren as they splashed the water of a blown up swimming pool.

She developed a close relationship with Coco the pet Maltese Shih Tzu. She always had a love for dogs especially her own sheepdogs: Max, Lassie and Floss. Now she was quite content to pat and praise Coco. In fact, she was a great source entertainment for her. She would laugh out loud when Coco jumped on to her lap to seek her attention and licked her fingers. Coco never growled when mum arrived.

It was not just her children, grandchildren, and Coco that she enjoyed conversing with. O no. On arrival to her family home in Creevyquin from the nursing home, her first port of call was to stop and chat to her mare and foal in the field just to the rear of our family home. Sitting in her wheelchair, the mare and foal would immediately race down the field to her, known to us as Gart Mór. They would lean their head over the white wrought iron gate waiting for mum as we helped her slowly to get out of the car. Seated then in her wheelchair, she didn't have to stretch too far to rub their mane gently as these two affectionate animals would lean their long necks over the gate to get closer to her. She would pat and praise them and called them by name. They would sniff her hand hoping that she would have some treats of a slice bread or maybe a small juicy apple for them to eat. It was obvious to mum and her daughters that the mare and foal greatly missed her presence and she missed them too.

Unfortunately, these activities are now a distant memory. Our mum no longer has the luxury of sitting beside the open fire, instead she sits beside the nursing home window looking out, waiting for her daughters to visit her for short-allocated periods of time. Precious time is spent communicating our lives and mum's friends lives through videos and photographs. WhatsApp and Viber have become a lifesaver for her. Mum smiles and her eyes open wide when her daughters arrive with fresh out of the oven homemade baking. And she loves when Coco pops up on the windowsill to wag her tail at her. Hellos and goodbyes are now unfortunately confined to blown kisses or outstretched arms through the narrow-opened window of the nursing home.

'I Love you Because...'

I am dedicating this memoir to everyone who cares for our mothers and fathers in a hospital, nursing home or family home setting. I am dedicating this memoir especially to Margaret Fannon, Breda O'Malley, Celina Fernández da Silva Ramos and Marion Heneghan to thank them for all the care and attention they gave to my dear mother.

We all know a song that reminds us of a special person, a special moment or a special time in our life. It may remind us of our teenage years, when we fell in love, got married or the birth of a child. We can remember where we were, what we were doing and who we were with. We may remember the month, the date and sometimes the actual time of the event.

There is one song that I have held in my memory since I was a child and will continue to hold onto it for my lifetime. It is a song that reminds me of my late mother who passed away recently. It's a song that makes me smile and cry. That song is called "I Love You Because." It got to number one in the Irish charts in the Spring of 1964. It was a hit for the well-known late country American singer, Jim Reeves. That same year, my amazing mother Marie came to the town of Roscommon to take up employment in Heaton's drapery store. Also, better still, it was the year she met dad.

I often wondered why she loved that song so much as she would always burst into song whenever she heard it playing on the radio. Many years ago, out of curiosity, I asked her why she liked the song so much. It was then, she admitted that it was the song that she sang in dad's ear while they were courting. Their courting days began back in June 1964. I found out the exact date shortly after she passed away when I began reading through her teal blue pocket size diary. She kept it hidden in the bottom drawer of her bedroom dressing room table. On Sunday, June 21st she wrote, "I met Roger."

Not only did I find her old diary, I also came across what I believed to be a love letter to my late father. However, upon opening it, I found out that it contained the lyrics of the song "I Love You Because" handwritten by my mother. I began to read the lyrics slowly and certain lines of the song stood out for me.

"You're always there to lend a helping hand, dear."

My siblings and I were blessed to have had such a caring mother who was always there to give us a helping hand. She was a home maker. She didn't work outside the home. Instead, she devoted her married life to rearing her five children and helping her husband on our busy dairy farm. She brought us wherever we needed to go. She had us spoilt, cleaning, cooking, washing and baking for us. She entertained everyone who came to visit our home or who came to work on our farm continuously for years.

She didn't confine her caring and selfless nature to her family. She was always there to help those who were sick and in need in our local community by paying regular visits to our elderly neighbours, residents and patients in our local nursing homes and our local Co. hospital. She is especially remembered by friends, neighbours and those in our community who have devotion to St Padre Pio. For over 30 years, my mother made annual Christmas visits in her local town, blessing people with Saint Padre Pio's glove who were hoping to receive some form of healing or miracle after touching it.

I always believed that the lyrics of this gentle, soft love song were written by Jim Reeves however I was wrong as I recently researched its history. I discovered that the song was written years earlier in 1949 by an American country songwriter call Leon Roger Payne. By researching the song, I came across a couple of surprising coincidences. Payne's second name Roger was also my late father's name and I also found out that when his wife Myrtle passed away, he had "I Love You Because" played at her funeral.

I had been playing that song religiously for the whole month of July 2021 for mum when I paid my visits to her in a private ward of a Galway hospital before she passed away. I was so thankful and blessed I got the chance to sit close to her for the first time in fifteen months. No longer did I have to speak to her through a half-closed window of a nursing home for a brief period of time. I was always watching the clock. Now; I no longer had to do that. Instead, I was very grateful to have the opportunity to spend as many hours as I wished with my mother with no one to tell me my visiting time was over. I decided that I was going to make the most of these precious hours. I would do my best to make this time as special as possible and try and make up in some way for all the lost time when I was not allowed to be physically close to her.

Sitting close to her bedside, wearing my mask and plastic apron to protects us both from the cursed covid, I got the opportunity to do the simple ordinary loving things that any proud daughter would wish to do for wonderful mother. I was going to do try with great difficulty to sooth and calm my ailing mother who was enduring both physical and mental suffering. Using a small comb, I gently combed her tossed hair on the pillow. I thought of all weekends down through the years, my mother was visited by her devoted hairdresser Marion. She came without fail every Saturday to our family home and to the nursing home where mum resided to cut and style her beautiful snow-white hair.

Having combed her hair gently, I would slowly and tenderly with my fore finger, cream her face with a fragranced face cream while she lay passively on the bed or in the orthopaedic chair. During such time, she managed to open her eyes briefly from time to time to look at me.

Having carried out both these tasks, I did what my mother would have done on a daily basis while she was in good health, I prayed with her. My mother was a devout catholic. As a young teenager of sixteen years, she became a member of the Children of Mary. In recent months, I found her Child of Mary medal hidden away in a purse among a collection of old coins. With squinting eyes, I eventually managed to read the tiny engraved letters on the back of the large silver medal. It read Marie Grogan, May 2nd, 1952, the date she joined the organization.

Every afternoon, that I spent with my mother in the hospital, I made sure that I had time to recite her favourite prayers with her which included the rosary and novenas to her two favourite saints. These saints, St. Padre Pio and St. Therese of Lisieux have provided many miraculous healings to our family down through the years. For the first couple of weeks of her stay in hospital, my mother managed to recite some of the prayers with me however as the weeks passed, her voice weakened. Instead, I continued to pray aloud for I knew that she was still listening.

After completing our daily prayers, it was then time to turn on YouTube on my phone. I made it my business to bring along my phone charger so that we would have plenty of time to listen to some good old classic songs that I heard my mother sing along to over the years. She always had the radio playing away on the kitchen counter close to the Stanley range and the electric cooker while she was cooking and baking.

"What will I play for you mum today," I would ask her even though I knew that she too week answer me. I scrolled down through the list of showband videos of the 1950s and 1960s on my phone. I knew who her favourite cabaret artists were and the special songs she sang along to over and over again down through the years. Sonny Knowles, "I'll take care of your Cares," was the song he always sang before leaving the stage each night. Brendan Boyer's hit "The Hucklebuck," was the number one hit for all of February 1965. That was the month that mum and dad got engaged. Dicky Rock's, ballad "From the Candy Store on the Corner" and Ruby Murray's, theme tune "Softly, Softly," was played too. She would have appreciated any song from Jim Reeves however "I love you Because" was the one love song I played for her every afternoon I was with her in hospital. A feeling of peace seemed to descend over her as I played these memorable songs. These were the songs that she once danced to in the many ballrooms built by the Reynold brothers from Longford.

On one day only, she took me by surprise when she recited all the lyrics of Dickie's hit "From the Candy Store on the Corner" as I played it for her. I was amazed that she could remember them all. Those few minutes stay with me as it was last time that my mum spoke the words of any song. I decided to research the history behind this song and the singer just as I had already researched Jim Reeves "I Love You Because." And yes, when I did my research, again, I found more coincidences. "From the Candy Store on the Corner was first released by Bob Hilliard into the chart in 1956 on August 18th. The 18th of August, was the date that mum and dad got married. Dickie released his version of the song in 1965. That was the year my parents got married.

This was another sweet song that my mother and father loved to dance to during the early years of their married life. It's no wonder she never forgot the words of "Candy Store." Other songs that mum loved to sing and that I had totally forgotten about included Nat King Cole's version of "Rambling Rose" and "A white Sport coat and a Pink Carnation" written by Marty Robbins. These songs were recently brought to my attention after seeing both artists perform them on television. To quench my curiosity, I decided I would enter both these songs into Wikipedia. I could not believe the coincidence once again. "A White Sports Coat and a Pink Carnation was released on April 20th 1957, my mother's 21st birthday. If only I had known that a few months early, I would definitely have played it over and over to her too. However, it was Jim Reeves and Dickie Rock who were her idols.

My family and I felt it was only fitting that her two favourite romantic ballads should be played at her funeral. As soon as "I love you Because" began to play out through the microphone, at my mother's graveside, the heavy rain that continuously fell that August bank holiday morning suddenly disappeared. Instead, the sun began to beam down on us, a sign maybe from my mother to let her family, friends and neighbours know that she was listening and singing along too.

Even though she is no longer with us physically, we will always find comfort from listening to the lyrics of this song and "I know" mum "your love will always see me through."

The last line of the song more importantly sums up why I truly adored my mother.

"But most of all I love you 'cause you're you."

'A Photo to Treasure'

Dedicated to Orla Faragher

As I sat in the heated passenger seat of our car beside my dear husband, a text message came through from my good friend, Orla.

"Are you on way back home from your weekend break yet?" the message read.

"Yes, we have decided to pull into your local Tesco's to do some shopping. I will send you a text to meet you in the car park when we arrive," I replied.

"Brilliant," came her rapid response. I knew she was anxious to meet me. We didn't get the opportunity to meet up since my dear mum passed away a few months earlier.

My husband and I had just parked the car when I spotted her jeep approaching us. She parked close to us. Both of us rushed out to greet each other. It was then we realised we couldn't even hug each other due to the covid variants that had taken over our world depriving us of some of our basic needs.

"Isn't it just awful that I can't even give you a decent hug after all you have been through," she said.

Orla was very vigilant when it came to hygiene. She was obsessed with washing and sanitising her hands and changing her mask on a regular basis so I wasn't prepared to let her stand outside on such a biting cold dark winter's evening. I invited her immediately to sit into the back seat of our car for a chat while my husband set off to do our weekend shopping.

"I have something for you," she said eagerly, and swiftly pulled out a square shaped gift, covered in bright colourful wrapping paper from a canvas bag. She handed it to me between the seats. At first, I thought it was a box of chocolates, however upon handling it, I knew it couldn't be due to its hard texture. I quickly pulled off the wrapping paper. I could not help but smile. It was a photo of my late mother and I. Orla had mounted it onto a wooden block. A very unique photo too as it was the only photo that was ever taken of my mother and I in the sitting room at our family home.

"I knew you would love it," Orla stated excitedly as she looked at the expression on my face.

"Do you remember when that was taken?" she asked me.

Of course, I could remember. It was almost two years since Orla came to visit my mum and I in our family home in Roscommon for the first time. She was on her way back from a visit to her own home town of Castlebar.

Not only was it the first time for Orla to visit our home, it was the first time ever that my mother got the opportunity to 'sink' into the mustard yellow patterned high-backed armchair that I had pulled up quite close to the dark mahogany fireplace that November evening. It was the first time in years that a fire was lit in the sitting room fireplace. However, that evening, I ensured that the fire blazed away as I continued to refuel the fire grate with logs and briquettes to keep my frail mother warm and cosy. Orla was amazed that our sitting room was left idle for so long.

"It's the truth, Orla. The only time my mother ever entered this room was to polish, dust and hoover. She took great pride in her dark mahogany furniture which she had purchased at various auctions during the 1980s. She also, always kept her EPNS silver trays, teapots, trophies and cups which she had won for Tennis well-polished. Our sitting room was kept more like a museum to admire, than a place to relax."

I took another long look at the photo. Mum was wearing a very special neck scarf containing the warm autumn colours of brown, orange and gold with a chocolate brown fringe on the ending. There was a story behind the scarf which I wanted to share with Orla.

"Orla, this scarf is very sentimental to me. A few years ago, mum informed me that she had originally bought the scarf for my late dad."

I could not imagine my father ever wearing a silk neck scarf. I had never seen him wear one even though my father had a great eye for fashion when it came to shirts, ties and suits. In later years, my mother began to wear the scarf herself on special occasions. And now I am getting great comfort when I wear the vintage neck scarf.

"It's a scarf that I won't be giving away to anyone not even you, Orla," I told her.

"I know exactly how you feel. You are like myself, a real sentimentalist!"

"Now tell me where are you thinking of placing the precious photo?" she asked me with curiosity.

"Well, I was thinking of standing it on top of the mantel piece in the sitting room in the family home," I answered quickly.

"Ah no, you will have to put that photo somewhere special

in your own home Evelyn so that you can look at both of you every day smiling happily. It will help you remember the treasured times you had with your marvellous mother."

"You are right Orla, I wasn't thinking," I admitted.

Suddenly, the ideal place to stand the cherished photo jumped into my head. I told her I would place it on the shelf in my kitchen where I could watch the two of us daily as I sat and dined at my kitchen table.

"That's more like Evelyn," Orla replied with contentment.

As the emotional meeting came to an end, I thanked her for her kind and thoughtful present. We promised each other that it would not be long before we would meet again and hoped that it wouldn't be the first and last time for her to come to visit me in my family home in Roscommon.

'Related To a Bishop'

Dedicated to my cousin John Killeen

I always knew that I was a related to him. My grandmother Margaret Killeen's maidan name was Gillooly and so, for many years, I thought he was her uncle. However, after researching the family tree, I found out that her father Timothy and her grandfather John Gillooly both resided in Stonepark, Roscommon whereas Lawrence was born in Gallowstown Roscommon. I eventually found out that this intelligent, ambitious yet humble man was her father's first cousin and Laurence's older brother who was a priest was also called Timothy. There were many things I didn't know about him until I started researching.

For over 50 years, I have walked through the main door of the Sacred Heart Church in Roscommon not realising that my ancestor Bishop Laurence Gillooly is to be seen holding a map on the tympanum, the triangular decorated mosaic which is to be viewed above that door. In fact, the Sacred Heart Church was built in his memory. Inside the church, in a stained-glass window situated between the confessional boxes and the statue of St. Therese of Lisieux, there is a depiction of him.

I wanted to find out more about this man. It is thanks to the recent publication of a book called "Dictionary of Irish Biography" that I found out about his wonderful achievements in the town of Athlone and Sligo during his prestigious career.

He was a fantastic administrator and a talented man who took on numerous tasks. It was he who instituted a system of regular clerical inspection of schools. I am very proud to say that he was the man who was responsible for the founding of Summerhill College in Athlone. And it was he who appointed his older brother Timothy to be the first president of the college.

While he was famously known as the Bishop of Elphin from 1856 until his death in 1895, he could have devoted his career to architecture or engineering for he took on the brave and huge responsibility of overseeing the construction of many churches, parochial residences, convents, schools and teacher's accommodation. It was he who over saw the building of the present Cathedral of the Immaculate Conception in Sligo town. He even had an input into the design of the building despite having no qualifications in Architecture.

From reading about this very hard-working man in the dictionary, I have come to believe that my ancestor was a man of no airs and graces. He was a bishop and was still willing to help out on a construction site and 'handle a wheel barrow' when he had much more responsibilities. He gave a hundred percent to all projects so much so that it caused him ill health.

Not only was he hardworking, he was humble and a man who wished to live a very simple life style. He refused to call his residence a palace instead referred to it as a presbytery. At his months' mind mass, Bishop Francis McCormack of Galway

(1837-1909) informed the congregation that he spent only one fifth of his income on his own personal needs. The rest of his money was given away to charities and to works going on in the diocese. Most of all, he was a man of prayer, spending hours each evening in spiritual reading.

When I think of him, I think of my father Roger who had the same work ethic. A man who worked on the farm from the early hours of the morning, a man who built many of the buildings still to be seen on our farm today and a man who did not believe in wasting time. Like his ancestor before him, he was out to achieve what he could in order to develop and run a successful farm to help support his family. He was also a generous man who helped out not only his own family but also his neighbours and friends in their times of need. He was definitely a devout man too. My father never let an evening pass without praying the rosary with his young family. He had great devotion to St. Padre Pio and received many healings through the saint's intercession.

In an article, describing the ordination of Father Kevin Doran, the present bishop of Elphin, I was delighted to read that the bishop's crozier is known as Gillooly's crosier. Bishop Doran remarked that the crozier was first used over 150 years ago by Bishop Lawrence Gillooly. He also stated that it was Bishop Gillooly who "led a period of great renewal in the diocese of Elphin."

Having found out that Bishop Lawrence was responsible for the building of the Sligo Cathedral, I now guessed he must be buried in the vicinity. It was Patrick Comerford's online description of the cathedral that led me to the exact spot of his burial. He is buried in the crypt beneath the baptistry which is located at the rear of the main altar.

I can no longer say I don't know much about Bishop Laurence Gillooly. What I can say is that I am very pleased that he is an ancestor of mine.

'Visit to Auntie Essie'

Dedicated to auntie Essie's sons; Ray, Phil, Mike, Bren and Ken.

Evelyn stands outside the red bricked terraced two-storey house and rings the doorbell, not once, twice but three times. There is no sign of auntie. Auntie Essie is, however, expecting her. She peers through the side window of the hall door and sees the sun peering faintly at the end of the corridor. She immediately guesses that she is out in the garden. She calls her house phone and waits. Suddenly, she sees her petite frame running through the long corridor. Evelyn stops ringing.

"It's only me, no need to rush," she calls out.

The door opens and she is greeted by auntie who has a flushed faced and is out of breath.

"Evelyn, you're looking marvellous." And then they hug.

"I was in the garden," she announces and follows with a quick order.

"Come with me," she says still breathing heavily.

She senses that her auntie's face is not flushed from relaxing in the sunshine on her white wrought iron bench in the back garden. Evelyn follows her quick footsteps through her extended kitchen while holding a fragrant rose bush in her arms. They walk over her new Navan patterned carpet. Auntie Essie has always had a carpet on her kitchen floor. This same kitchen acted as her Montessori classroom for two decades.

From her kitchen, her colourful garden is observed through the wall-to-wall glass double doors. They enter the garden, feeling the melting May sun shower onto their faces. Her guess is correct. She hasn't been relaxing. She has been cutting the grass. Evelyn spots the old-fashioned push lawnmower.

"I haven't seen one of them since I was a…"

"I'll finish this first and then I'll talk to you Evelyn because I can no longer multi task," she replied interrupting her in mid-sentence.

A square shaped piece of grass waits to be cut. Auntie Essie begins to mow. Evelyn does not offer to mow the grass for this very independent woman. This spritely lady, just ninety years young has admitted on many occasions that the garden means so much to her. She stands and admires her auntie's energy as she pushes the lawn mower over and back. Now and again, she kicks the blades to release the excess grass that sticks. The square piece of grass eventually disappears. She, then, moves the lawnmower underneath the antique bench. Evelyn recalls auntie telling her that the same bench was excavated from beneath the garden when renovating it many 'moons ago'.

She completes the job and places the lawnmower safely back in the shed towards the rear of the garden. Evelyn eventually gets the opportunity to present her with the rose bush. The deep pink fragrant rose is called "Bright as A Button" reflecting auntie's personality. It is a belated birthday present. Auntie immediately takes the rose bush from her and carefully chooses a suitable spot for it to grow. She makes her decision.

"I will plant it here in front of the large palm tree," placing it on the freshly cut grass.

"Would you like me to sow it for you later," Evelyn asks.

"Not at all, I have plenty of time to sow it myself."

And then quickly invites Evelyn back into her kitchen.

"You must be starving, after your long journey. You'll have a toasty and a cup of tea," she insists.

Evelyn doesn't argue with auntie. She doesn't ask to help her make the tea, boil the kettle or set the table. She is the host and Evelyn is the guest. This is a tradition that she has kept up since she started having visitors as a newly wed to her south side home in the mid-1950s. Evelyn sits at the rectangle mahogany table as she prepares the toasty. Pink and black squared tablemats are in place to save the table from marks or stains. The toasty is soon ready and placed in front of her. All she has to do is pour the Lyons tea from auntie Essie's China tea pot. The conversations, like the tea, begin to 'pour out'.

Everyone from Essie's late husband, her brothers and sisters who have all since passed away are spoken about with great affection. News about her sons, nephews, nieces and neighbours are revealed too. She also takes great interest in Evelyn's family. Some of the stories have become milestones in her life, impacting on her greatly. It makes her the woman she is today. Auntie loves to repeat some of these true stories each time she visits. Auntie usually surprises her during each visit with a new revelation.

On this occasion, Evelyn has a surprise revelation for her as she begins to read an article to her from the New York Post newspaper dated January 1936. It describes the execution of four young men who were sent to the electric chair for shooting a patrolman who tried to prevent them from robbing a leather goods shop on Fifth Avenue, New York. That patrolman was auntie's cousin James. As Evelyn reads the story, auntie listens carefully. Suddenly, she interrupts to state "Isn't that extraordinary." This is a line she repeats quite often. She informs Evelyn that the article she is reading to her has been read to her before. Auntie recalls vividly her mother sitting in her family childhood kitchen in Creevyquin reading the same article in front of a young Essie, a child then of just seven years.

"Mammy read the shocking news to daddy while he was sitting at the table eating his dinner and I remember she burst into tears as she read it. Mammy could feel the pain too of those four mothers who lost their sons to death in the electric chair for they were far too young to die."

"The kitchen is getting cold," she exclaims suddenly.

Evelyn feels that it's an event that auntie does not want to dwell on.

"You head up to the front sitting room while I set the table for the breakfast. You can turn on the electric fire. It will heat up the room in minutes," she states.

On arrival, Evelyn immediately scans the room. A collection of 90th birthday cards sit on the mahogany coffee table close to the fireside armchair. However, there is something else that greatly interests her.

"Where is it? it's always on the carpeted floor next to the fireplace." she mutters to herself.

It is a framed black and white photo taken in the early 1900s. It is a photo of Evelyn's grandmother, Essie's mother. It is a precious photo for it is the only one auntie has in her possession of her mother as a young single woman in her early twenties. Her secret wish is every time she goes to visit her that auntie will offer it to her. The photo however is no longer there. Evelyn does not have the courage to ask her where is it. 'She must have given it away to a family member,' she whispers to herself.

Suddenly, auntie appears at the sitting room door.

"Did you not turn on the fire yet," she asks Evelyn.

"O no, I was busy reading these lovely cards you got for your birthday," she lies.

"Really, you weren't looking for anything else, by any chance?" smiling.

"What do you mean Essie?"

"Hold on a minute now."

Auntie walks over to the forest green couch and picks up a brown canvas bag with strong handles on it.

"Were you looking for this by any chance?"

Evelyn opens up the bag to find a parcel in the shape of a rectangle.

"Go on, open it," instructs auntie.

Evelyn unwraps the floral paper carefully to reveal the photo of her young grandmother.

"O auntie, I thought you had given it to someone when I didn't see it sitting on the carpet."

"Well, I noticed that each time you came to visit you admired it, so I decided that I would give it you on your next visit. Sure, you deserve it and I know you will treasure it, Evelyn."

They both take a long look at the black and white photo of their ancestor. Essie's mother Margaret, has dense dark eyebrows just like both of them. Her hair is dark and wavy tied up in a bun with a ribbon. While all three of them are very dark and sallow, they are not blessed with granny's fine head of wavy hair.

"There is an extraordinary resemblance between the three of us no doubt," remarks auntie.

"I read once that people with broad dense eyebrows form great friendships and like new beginnings. If that is so auntie, you and I take after granny Margaret."

"I agree with you there."

"While we are on the subject of photos, do you know what we should do tomorrow morning?"

"What?" asks auntie.

"We must take some photographs of the two of us out in that beautiful garden of yours."

Essie's alarm clock goes off at 8.00am. She sets it for that time every morning so that she can take her time to get ready for mass.

"Will we go to mass?" Essie asks Evelyn as she peeps her head around the bedroom door the following morning.

They both look at each other with tired eyes.

"I think we'll skip it for today, sure we're not long in bed. You kept me up 'till all hours as usual!"

She leaves to go back to her own bedroom but not for long as her head peeps once again around the corner of the bedroom door.

"Well on second thoughts, we might as well get up now and make the most of the bright sunny day that's in it."

The sun blazes in through the large sliding door as they have their breakfast consisting of porridge made on water the night before. This is followed by tea, toast and marmalade. The making of the porridge is a tradition that Evelyn's own mother has kept going down through the years.

After breakfast, auntie gets up from the breakfast table and enters the small bathroom next to the kitchen. Evelyn secretly stands at a distance. She observes auntie in admiration. Essie applies moisturiser and foundation to her youthful face and neck in the mirror over the peach-coloured wash hand basin. Then, holding a hand-held mirror, she strokes her faded eyebrows with eye brow pencil that was once jet black just like her mother before her.

"Are you ready yet?" Evelyn teases.

"No, I need to do something with my neck," she answers.

When it comes to looking after one's appearance, Auntie Essie is the lady who continues to look her best no matter what the occasion is. She pulls open the corner press in the kitchen which contains an array of scarves of different colours, textures and styles. After a quick glide of her eye, she settles on an ivory and black polka dot neck scarf to match her black and white cotton jumper. She returns to the bathroom to look into the mirror and neatly ties the knot in the scarf to the side of her neck.

"Now I'm ready," she announces and then waltzes back into the kitchen.

Then they enter her back garden full of roses, lilies and agapanthuses. The purple agapanthus flowers are as tall as auntie and form a colourful background for any photo. They grow close to the bird table where auntie decides to stand to have her photograph taken. She stands with her shoulders held back. It makes her slight frame of five foot two seem much taller. Evelyn takes her photo and then takes a long look at it.

'This is a photo that I will be framing, 'she thinks to herself. Selfies of them both are taken too.

"I will print the photos and post them to you shortly," Evelyn promises her as she takes her leave at her classical style hall door.

"Thank you again for the photo of granny," she adds and kisses her auntie's soft cheek before opening the white wrought iron gate.

"You are most welcome Evelyn. God bless and safe home," she calls out as she watches her walk away down the avenue.

Evelyn does not say good bye to auntie. She doesn't like goodbyes. Instead she tells her she will phone her soon.

'My Gifted Godmother'

Dedicated to auntie Carmel's daughters and sons: Maureen, Paul, John and Grainne.

We are all gifted with godmothers when we are christened. A godmother's responsibility is to support, care and take interest in their godchild during their childhood and teenage years if the need arises. I believe I was born with an extra special godmother. She provided me with wonderful support, great advice and took a deep interest in my life until just a few weeks before she passed away.

Auntie Carmel was my gifted godmother, my mother's oldest sister. She was born in the town of Moate Co. Westmeath. It was in that town, she lived all her life, marrying the son of the local well-known publican Peter Egan. The family name is still retained over the bar door and is located on Main Street, Moate since it was established in 1854.

My godmother was a petite lady, always soft spoken with a

gentle manner. She was blessed with a thoughtful heart and was a very proud mother of two daughters and two sons.

In her youth, she was an active and talented sportswoman, participating in many tennis matches on the local Carmelite college lawns. In later years, she became a skilful golf player and was at one stage given the title 'lady captain' of Moate golf club.

From an early age, she had a great love for antiques especially antique furniture just like my own mother and would spend many weekends travelling around the country to auctions purchasing various items that took her fancy. She was so fascinated with these antiques that she decided to set up her own business in her home town. She named it "Any Ould Thing" and was suitably located beside her husband's bar.

As I mentioned earlier, she had been very thoughtful. She never forgot my birthday or my mother's birthday. She didn't just send us ordinary shop bought cards. No, her cards were unique and creative. She put great effort into them. She would cut out funny verses, poems, pictures that she kept from old magazines and greeting cards and then stuck them onto coloured cards, creating her own distinctive design. Her cards were always amusing and from time to time she included her own drawings of cute animals or colourful flowers on the greeting card.

Not only did she send us greeting cards, she sent us mass bouquets too. Auntie Carmel was a devout catholic. She believed in the power of prayer and the importance of attending mass on a daily basis. She would pray for anyone who needed help. Throughout her life, she battled her own various illnesses. By praying to her favourite saints, St. Therese, the little flower, St. Padre Pio and Our lady, she always recovered quickly. Statues and religious pictures adorned every room in her home. She often remarked to me that she frequently received the strong smell of roses while praying to these saints and believed it was a sign that her prayers would be answered.

I looked forward to my frequent visits to her home over the years. Sitting in her Dartmouth green coloured kitchen, across from each other at her kitchen table, we listened to each other's news and views. She was willing to give me sound advice whenever I needed it. For many years, I brought my mother with me to visit her before the cursed covid took over and deprived the close sisters of their precious time together. The friendly visit would always include a cup of tea served with her tasty homemade brown bread followed by apple tart. Sometimes she provided us with a variety of cakes to choose from. These were taken out of a biscuit box that she stored in her kitchen larder.

On many visits, I enjoyed being invited into her art room. Auntie Carmel had discovered she had another hidden talent in her later years when she decided to take up art lessons. Over time, she became a competent and confident artist. On one occasion, she brought out her latest piece of art work to the kitchen for my mother and I to view. It was a seascape with a red and white paddle boat sitting on the sandy beach close to the shore with clumps of seaweed lying close by. We were both amazed by what she had achieved after just two nights working on the canvas. Her art room contained all her paintings and decorated the four walls of what was once a bedroom. She had transformed it into an art gallery. Apart from seascapes and landscapes, she also enjoyed painting dogs, foxes, cats and birds. I was delighted when during one visit she asked me to choose a painting as a gift for my new home. I decided to choose a landscape scene of an azure blue sky with cloud cover which complimented a deep blue lake surrounded by a high sun speckled mountain to the left and a forest walk to the right. This precious piece of art personally signed by her, now hangs in my hallway.

During my summer visits to her, she would always invite me out to see her large walled garden. She was very proud of her garden, a place that brought her contentment and peace especially during the last couple of years of her life. She spent many days there tending to her roses and hydrangeas. She loved roses. I noticed that she always had some freshly cut roses sitting in a vase on her kitchen window sill during my visits.

As well as regular visits to auntie Carmel, we kept in regular contact by phone. And if I forgot to call her, she would show her concern by phoning me to find out if I was ok.

While those enjoyable visits and phone calls have come to an end and her humorous handmade cards no longer come through my letterbox due to her recent death, I feel blessed to have had her in my life. She was truly a gifted lady with many talents, but most of all I admired her gift of kindness. May she rest in peace.

In memory of

my loving father and mother
Roger and Marie Killeen
and
My godmother, Carmel Egan

Dedicated to Fergal
And all the relatives of the Killeen and Grogan families, especially Essie Killeen Aherne, Nollaig Grogan Kelly, PJ and Mossie Grogan.
Also, my neighbours and friends especially those whom I wrote a poem to celebrate a special day in their lives.

Acknowledgements:

I would like to thank the following publications and their respective editors where many of my short stories and memoirs appeared for the first time:

'Roscommon Champion', 'Roscommon People', 'Roscommon Herald,' 'Ireland's Eye,' 'Ireland's Own,' 'Writing.ie,' 'Woman's Way' and The Voice of Padre Pio magazine.'

I would like to thank Fergal, my family and friends in Limerick, Clare and Roscommon for all their support and encouragement. Having enjoyed reading my stories, poems and memoirs, they motivated me to bring this book to fruition.

I would like to thank Orla Faragher for her patience and help with the editing of some of my short stories.

I would like to thank my cousin Gillian Egan who created the beautiful illustration for the front cover of "I Love You Because."

And lastly, I would like to thank Dr. Niall MacGiolla Bhuí at TheDocCheck.com who provided me with excellent advice and support during the preparations leading up to the publication of "I Love you Because."

Biography

Evelyn Killeen McCrann was born in Creevyquin just outside Roscommon town. She now resides in Co. Clare. Evelyn attended University College Galway as a mature student to study an Arts Degree in English and Physical Geography followed by a Higher Diploma in Education.

Evelyn qualified as a secondary school teacher in 2002, however she has devoted her career to special education since 2006. It was at this time that her interest in writing short stories, poetry and memoirs began to flourish.

In 2020, her sentimental and humorous short story "The Importance of Waiting" was short listed for The Roscommon New Writing Award.

She writes about some of her extraordinary, unforgettable and enjoyable times growing up on the family farm. She also writes about the wonderful friendships she has developed, kept and renewed since her school days and up through the years to the present day.

Many of her poems have been written for special occasions.

'I Love You Because'...is Evelyn's debut book which may bring a tear to your eye.